JOSEPH CHALMERS, O.CARM.
PRIOR GENERAL

MARY, THE CONTEMPLATIVE

JOSEPH CHALMERS, O.CARM.
PRIOR GENERAL

MARY, THE CONTEMPLATIVE

EDIZIONI CARMELITANE
ROMA, 2001
MARIAN CARMELITE YEAR

© Edizioni Carmelitane
Via Sforza Pallavicini, 10
00193 Roma, Italia

ISBN: 88-7288-070-X

CONTENTS

CHAPTER ONE

THE BEGINNINGS

The year 2001 was very significant for all Carmelites, being, according to a venerable tradition, the 750th anniversary of the beginning of the scapular devotion. This year was marked by celebrations all over the world but also of course mixed with great sorrow due to the terrorist attacks in the USA on the eve of the public audience of the Carmelite Family with the Pope. The Carmelite Family was honoured to receive a letter from Pope John Paul II to mark the Marian year.[1] In this letter, the Pope noted that for Carmel this was "a marvellous occasion to deepen not only its Marian spirituality, but to live it more and more in the light of the place that the Virgin Mother of God and our Mother occupies in the mystery of Christ and the Church."[2]

The reason for this work is to honour Mary's place in Carmel and to examine some of the implications of this Marian spirituality for the spiritual journey. There are very many approaches one could take to the topic of Our Lady in Carmelite spirituality. The Pope presents two essential aspects of Carmelite Marian spirituality in his letter: "For the members of the Carmelite Family, Mary, the Virgin Mother of God and Mother of all people, is not only a model to imitate but is also present as Mother and Sister in whom one can confide."[3]

One approach that would seem to be very fruitful especially for our days is Mary as the one who listened to the Word of God.[4] Mary listened to the Word of God and put it into practice. (cf. Lk. 8,19-21) Through her the Word was made flesh. (cf. Jn.1,14) If we want to have a real devotion to Our Lady, we must also listen to the Word and welcome it into our lives. The Word will change us radically.

First of all, let us take a brief look at how devotion to Our Lady developed within Carmel.[5] Not a lot is known about the first hermits

---

[1] See Appendix I for the letter in full.

[2] *Letter of Pope John Paul II*, 25th March 2001, para 1

[3] *Ibid*, para 3

[4] See Talk by Fr. Sandro Vella O.Carm. given at Carmelite Family Day in Aylesford, England on 20th May 2001, at http://www.carmelite.org/laycarmel/marycontemplative.htm, part of the web site of the British Province of the Carmelite Order

[5] For a full treatment of this subject, see E. Boaga, *The Lady of the Place*, Edizioni Carmelitane, Rome, 2001.

on Mount Carmel who stand at the beginning of the Carmelite Order.[6] What is known is that between the years 1206 and 1214 these men from Western Europe, who had desired to dedicate their lives to Jesus Christ in his own land, had achieved sufficient cohesion among themselves to desire to receive some official recognition from the Church of their association. It was decided to approach Albert, the Patriarch of Jerusalem, to ask him to write for them a "formula vitae" (rule of life). Albert wrote a letter to the hermits[7] describing how they were to live their lives. In composing this rule for the hermits, Albert took into account their avowed purpose, which was "to live a life of allegiance to Jesus Christ".[8] In Chapter 14 of this short document, Albert lays down that the hermits are to build an oratory in the middle of the cells where they are to gather for mass each morning.[9]

In the 13th century the naming of a church was a very important event and especially so when the church belonged to a specific group. The feudal system was in operation at the time, which meant that people bound themselves to a particular lord or baron whom they would serve and who in turn had the duty to protect them. The feudal lord would bind himself to the king and include all those who had taken an oath of fealty to him. In the religious sphere a group would chose a saint to be their patron. The Carmelites named their oratory in honour of Our Lady, the "lady of the place". In this way they were binding themselves to her service and taking her as patroness. In the understanding of the age, she bound the hermits more closely to the service of Christ her Son, who was in a very particular way "the sovereign lord of the Holy Land". This act of taking Mary as patroness was the seed that was to flower into the Carmelite tradition of honouring the Mother of God.

The first phase of the Carmelite tradition with regard to Mary is to see her as patroness. The hermits had the duty to honour and serve her and they believed that she had the duty to protect them. It became increasingly difficult for Christians to remain in the Holy Land because of the Saracens who were pushing their frontiers ever

---

[6] See J. Smet, *The Carmelites: A History of the Brothers of Our Lady of Mount Carmel*, (Institutum Carmelitanum, Rome 1975), Vol. I

[7] K. Waaijman, *The Mystical Space of Carmel*, Peeters, Netherlands, 2000, especially for the literary form of the Rule. See also Appendix II for the Carmelite Rule in full.

[8] *Rule,1*

[9] *Rule*, 14

further. Around the 1230's the decision was taken that the hermits would leave the Holy Land for Europe, where they spread very quickly.

Conditions in Europe were not at all favourable to the way of life that the hermits desired to live. Various problems seemed to conspire against them. Albert, the Patriarch of Jerusalem, who had written the rule for the hermits, was murdered in 1214.[10] In the following year was held the Fourth Lateran Council during which it was decreed that no new religious orders could be founded. All new communities were to adopt either the Rule of St. Benedict or that of St. Augustine. The hermits made a direct appeal to the pope and in 1226 he gave a limited approval to their way of life. It became increasingly obvious that conditions in Europe were not conducive to an eremitical style of life and so in 1247 at a General Chapter held at Aylesford, in England, the Carmelites decided to join the new mendicant movement and become mendicant friars, like the Franciscans and Dominicans.

Despite the limited papal approval, the position of the Carmelites was still very insecure. The other orders saw them as rivals who had no right to exist. The Carmelites claimed to have a special relationship with Mary who was their patroness, mother and sister. Indeed it was claimed that the Carmelite Order had been founded for the praise and glory of Our Lady and that they were "the brothers of Our Lady of Mount Carmel"[11] This did not endear them to other religious orders who also claimed to have a devotion to Our Lady. At the Council of Lyons in 1274, the Franciscans and Dominicans were approved but the Carmelites were only allowed to remain in existence until a proper study of their "usefulness" could be undertaken.[12] In 1298 Pope Boniface VIII gave full approval to the Carmelites and he retroactively wrote this approval into the decrees of the Council of Lyons. Even this definitive acceptance of the Carmelites as a religious order did not end their difficulties. All these problems came to a head in 1374 at a debate in Cambridge, England. The purpose of the debate was to decide whether the Carmelites had the right to call themselves "brothers of the Blessed Virgin Mary". It

---

[10] For a full history of St. Albert, see V. Mosca, *Alberto Patriarca di Gerusalemme*, (Edizioni Carmelitane, Rome, 1996)

[11] A. Staring, *Medieval Carmelite Heritage*, (Institutum Carmelitanum, Rome, 1989), p. 44-48.

[12] J. Smet, , *The Carmelites: A History of the Brothers of Our Lady of Mount Carmel*, Vol. I, p. 17-18

was finally decreed that they had such a right and Pope Urban VI confirmed this in 1379. In his bull, the Carmelites are called, "The Order of the Blessed Mary, Mother of God, Our Lady of Mount Carmel".[13]

Liturgical Devotion

Carmelites honoured Mary especially in the liturgy.[14] Until the debate at Cambridge, the Carmelites had celebrated an ordinary commemoration of Our Lady of Mount Carmel. This mass was often held weekly and it was to thank Mary for her continued protection of the Order. After the victory at Cambridge, the Solemn Commemoration of Our Lady of Mount Carmel was instituted. It was felt that Our Lady had made sure that the Order would survive and therefore had indeed fulfilled her role as patroness. This Solemn Commemoration began in England on the 17th July. It very quickly spread to the rest of Europe and was fixed on the 16th July.

Before the Solemn Commemoration of Our Lady of Mount Carmel had been instituted, the principal feasts of Our Lady celebrated within the Order were variously the Annunciation, the Immaculate Conception and in England especially, the Assumption.[15] The Immaculate Conception, which was known as "the sanctification of Mary in the womb of St. Anne",[16] was instituted as a feast in 1306. In Rome the Carmelites invited the Roman Curia to their principal church to celebrate this feast as other orders did on their annual feast.[17]

The Second Vatican Council stressed that devotion to Mary be nurtured especially through the liturgy. When possible Carmelites still celebrate the ordinary commemoration of Our Lady of Mount Carmel on a Saturday and the 16th July is still held as the patronal feast of the whole Order under the title of the Solemn Commemo-

---

[13] Joseph de Sainte Marie, *La Vierge du Mt. Carmel*, (Éditions P. Lethielleux, Paris, 1985), p.180.

[14] L. Saggi, *Santa Maria del Monte Carmelo* in *Santi del Carmelo*, (Institutum Carmelitanum, Rome, 1972), p.116. See also English translation and abridged version, G. Pausback, *Saints of Carmel*, (Carmelite Institute, Rome, 1972).

[15] Joseph de Sainte Marie, *La Vierge du Mt. Carmel*, p.180

[16] L. Saggi, *Santa Maria del Monte Carmelo* p. 125

[17] Joseph de Sainte Marie, *La Vierge du Mt.Carmel*, p.180

ration of Our Lady of Mount Carmel. The emphasis in the prayers of the masses in honour of Our Lady of Mount Carmel is on her protection and her guidance towards Christ her Son. For example the prayer over the gifts for the solemnity puts it this way:- ".... In your service may our love become like hers and so unite us more closely with the work of redemption".[18] The office of readings for the solemnity contains an excerpt from the writings of a Carmelite mystic of the 17th century, Michael of St. Augustine. He explains what Marian devotion means:- "Whoever loves her as mother must strive to acquire her humility, her purity, her poverty, her obedience; to follow her in her love of God and her neighbour - in a word, in every virtue."[19]

Our Lady as Model

The liturgical devotion to Mary among the Carmelites affected how they understood their vocation. In 1287 at the General Chapter held in Montpellier, France, it was decided that the cloak which the Carmelites wore be changed from the original striped mantle to a pure white cloak. This was understood as a symbol of the virginity of Mary. One of the favourite titles for Mary among medieval Carmelites was "Most Pure Virgin". Mary's virginity was seen as a symbol of her total dedication to God with a pure heart. She was understood to epitomise the beatitude - "Blessed are the pure in heart". Carmelites, who had their roots in the eremitical tradition, sought this same total dedication and they saw in Mary all that they were striving to be.

Another major aspect of Mary that fascinated medieval Carmelites was the divine maternity. The Carmelites, as an Order with a strong contemplative thrust, sought union with God and no closer union could be thought of than Mary carrying the divine child in her womb. Although they were an Order with many active apostolates, the Carmelites never forgot their roots as hermits on Mount Carmel. The primary aspect of their vocation was often said to be contemplation, understood as the search for an intimate relationship of union with God. They sought the presence of God within them and in the midst of their activity. Mary was an inspiration for

---

[18] *The Carmelite Missal*, 1979)

[19] *Carmelite Proper of the Liturgy of the Hours*, (Institutum Carmelitanum, Rome, 1993), p. 165

them since she showed that close union with God was possible for a human being. She was called mother of Carmel in the sense that she nurtured the divine life within those who sought her aid. The Carmelites also thought of her as a sister because she had shared our life on earth and knew its ups and downs.[20]

The English Carmelite theologian, John Baconthorpe (d. 1348) tried to show that the Carmelite way of life was patterned on that of Mary.[21] He said that the Order was founded for the purpose of venerating her and he pointed out that the highest form of veneration is imitation.

One of the strongest formative influences on Carmelites from the 14th century until relatively recently was a collection of books edited by the Spanish Carmelite, Philip Ribot in 1370. This purports to be a collection of very early texts although at least some of them seem to have been written by Ribot himself. One of these books, entitled, "The Institution of the First Monks",[22] was thought at one time to pre-date the Rule written by Albert.

According to the times in which this book was written, the interpretation of Scripture was allegorical. The cloud, which the prophet Elijah saw (1 Kings 18, 41-46), was interpreted as a symbol of Mary immaculately conceived and bearing the saviour while remaining a virgin. Mary was understood to embody what every Carmelite strives for - to remove all trace of actual sin and to be transparent in order to allow God who dwells within to shine forth.[23]

A more modern Carmelite, Blessed Titus Brandsma, killed in Dachau in 1942 for openly opposing the Nazis, said that all Christians and especially Carmelites should be "other Marys" in the sense that just as Christ grew in her and came to birth, so must we allow the love of God to grow in us. Just as she was the "God-bearer" for the world, we too must bring God into every situation and be able to perceive the presence of God that is so often hidden by external realities. He also said that Carmelites are to prolong in the Church what God had worked in Mary. She was God's masterpiece. She had co-operated fully with God and therefore has given us an exam-

---

[20] *Letter of Superiors General of the Carmelite Orders, "With Mary the Mother of Jesus"*, 16 May, 2001.

[21] E. Boaga, *The Lady of the Place*, p.26-27

[22] A. Staring, *Medieval Carmelite Heritage*, p. 11-12

[23] E. Boaga, *The Lady of the Place*, p.50-51

ple of how to respond when God approaches - "Let it be done to me according to your word. (Lk 1, 38)[24]

Despite the fact that Our Lady is unlike us in that she was completely sinless and had a unique relationship with God, nevertheless Carmelites saw in her the fullest expression of what they aspired to be. They never saw her as distant or untouchable because of her privileges; instead, because of their traditional understanding of Our Lady as their Patroness, Mother and Sister, Carmelites always tended to have a close and intimate relationship with her.

The Scapular

From the late 14th century the brown scapular summed up Carmelite devotion to Mary. The scapular was a part of the Carmelite habit and probably originally served as an apron. There were various legends connected to religious habits in general in medieval times. Apparitions of the founder of the particular order or of Our Lady were frequently involved. It was related that Our Lady had appeared to Simon Stock, the Prior General of the Carmelites, in the year 1251, had taken hold of his scapular and promised that anyone who died wearing this garment would not perish eternally. There is little concrete historical evidence concerning the scapular vision of Simon Stock but there is "a venerable tradition"[25] of the Order in its regard. In any case, the symbolism of the scapular as a sign of consecration to Mary, the Mother of Carmel, was and remains very important. Very many people began to wear a miniature version of the scapular. Scapular societies were set up all over Europe and missionaries used the scapular as a catechetical tool wherever they went. The wearing of the scapular

---

[24] Cf. Bl. Titus Brandsma, *Lecture to the Marian Congress of Tangerloo*, August, 1936: *Carmelite Mysticism, Historical Sketches*, Chicago, 1936, Lecture IV, 52-53. "We ought not to think of imitation without thinking of union, nor of union without the thought of imitation. Each flows into the other, though one or other may be more emphasised at a particular time. We need to keep the two fused in a harmonious unity. If we wish to conform ourselves to Mary in order to enjoy fully a relationship with God according to her example, we must become other Marys. We must allow Mary to live in us. Mary must not be outside the Carmelite, who should live a life like that of Mary, living with, in, through and for Mary." Here, Bl. Titus is alluding to the Marian and Mariform life taught particularly by the Low Countries mystics, the Venerable Michael of St. Augustine (d. 1684) and the Venerable Mary of St. Teresa Petijt/Petyt (d. 1677).

[25] See *Letter of Pope John Paul II*, 25th March 2001, para 1

became so popular that by the end of the 16th century, for example Spain and Portugal were described as one immense Carmel.[26]

Many Carmelites through the centuries have written about the scapular. Arnold Bostius (1445-99) said that the wearing of the scapular is a commitment to live the virtues of Mary.[27] Mathias of St. John (d. 1681) piled up biblical examples of how God has used material things as instruments of grace. The scapular for him was one such material thing, which God could use for the benefit of humanity. However he insisted that wearing the scapular was no magic talisman. He wrote, "It would be far better to have holiness under a worldly habit than a worldly heart under a holy habit".[28]

Through the scapular the Carmelite family desired to share the gifts of God, and in a particular way, the maternal love of Mary, with all those who wished to be included. As Mary clothed her child in swaddling clothes when he was born, so she still takes care of Christ's body, the Church. The scapular is understood to be symbolic clothing signifying the protection of Mary for the one who wears it. A mother helps a child to grow up and so Mary also helps us to become what God knows we can be. A mother teaches her child especially by her example. At Cana she tells us, "Do whatever he tells you" (Jn. 2,5). By looking at her we learn what it means to be a follower of Christ.

The scapular is a reminder of Mary's commitment to us and our commitment to Mary. It is a reminder of her constant presence in our lives and her interest in us. She really is a Mother and a Sister, leading us and guiding us to Christ her Son in whom we find salvation. She is with us in life and in death. We say to her often, "Pray for us now and at the hour of our death". Pope John Paul wrote in regard to the scapular: "It is a sign of the continual protection of the Most Holy Virgin, not only throughout life but also at the moment of the transition towards the fullness of eternal glory."[29]

There are many sons and daughters of earthly mothers who make a big splash on Mother's Day with flowers and chocolates but who cannot be bothered with their mothers throughout the rest of the

[26] For an in depth study of the origins and development of the scapular devotion, see E. Boaga, *The Lady of the Place*, P. 93-118

[27] R. Valabek, *Mary Mother of Carmel* (Carmel in the World Paperbacks, Rome, 1988), Vol. 1, p. 76

[28] *Ibid.*, p.262

[29] *Letter of Pope John Paul II*, 25th March, para 5

year. Chocolates and flowers are very nice but if there is no regular contact to back them up, their significance gets watered down. Devotion must express itself in some way. If the outward signs of devotion emerge from a real relationship with Our Lady, then they have a deep significance. Jesus heavily criticised the Pharisees because of their outward displays of religion that had no basis in reality. If the outward signs are just a passing emotion, they will have no lasting impact on our lives. We show our devotion to Our Lady by living as she has shown us.

Wearing the scapular is intended to be an outward reminder of what should be going on within. The danger with any outward sign is that it remain merely outward and therefore the stress today is on the necessity of living what the scapular symbolises. Mary is seen to be the perfect example of what it means to follow Christ. The meaning of the scapular today can perhaps be summed up in one of the prayers over the people at the end of the mass of the Solemnity of Our Lady of Mount Carmel:- "Lord, grant that those who in devotion have put on the habit of Our Lady of Mount Carmel, may put on her virtues also and enjoy her unfailing protection".[30]

Mary in Carmel Today

Modern Carmelites are heirs to a long tradition with regard to Mary, the Mother of Jesus. The Second Vatican Council called for religious orders to return to their roots in order to find inspiration to renew themselves.[31] The primary source of renewal was to be found in the Gospel and secondarily in the beginnings of each religious family. Running throughout Carmelite history is a strong Marian flavour and a conviction that Carmel without Mary simply would not exist. In the formation document for the Carmelite Order,[32] Mary is seen as an inspirational figure. In her the Carmelites find the perfect image of all they desire and hope to be. Since she is the perfect disciple of the Lord, she is our sister on the journey of faith, leading us to the transforming encounter with God. She is our Mother encouraging us to look to her Son.

If we are true children of Mary, and her brothers and sisters, we

---

[30] *Carmelite Missal*

[31] *Perfectae Caritatis*, no. 2

[32] *Ratio Institutionis Vitae Carmelitanae, Carmelite Formation: a Journey of transformation*, (General Curia of the Carmelite Order, Rome, 2000), esp. nos. 44, 48-49

will be willing to learn from her. In St. John's Gospel, Our Lady plays a pivotal role. She does not appear very often but her appearances are at crucial times. She is present at the beginning of Jesus' public ministry at the marriage feast of Cana, and at the end of his public ministry at the foot of the cross, when she becomes the Mother of all believers. She is responsible for hastening the beginning of the public ministry, when she points out to her Son that "they have no wine". (Jn. 2, 3). Jesus tells her that it has nothing to do with him but she knows her Son very well; she is not put off by his words. In fact she goes to the servants and urges them to do whatever he tells them. We know that Jesus told them to fill the huge jars with water, which would have been a very laborious task. Some biblical expert has worked out that about 120 gallons of water were turned into wine that day! The servants did what Jesus told them to do, even though it must have seemed futile, and their obedience and faith in him were repaid a hundredfold.

Our Lady always points us to Jesus and continually reminds us to do whatever he tells us. Sometimes we may be tempted to think that what the Lord wants of us does not make much sense, like loving our neighbour and forgiving not seven times but seventy times seven and so on. However, if we seek to put the message of Jesus into practice day in and day out, we will discover that we will be repaid a hundredfold. God is never outdone in generosity.

From the cross, Jesus gave the beloved disciple to Our Lady to be her son. (Jn. 19, 25-27) The beloved disciple represents all Christians. All of us have been given into the care of Mary, our Mother. Equally, Jesus told the beloved disciple, representing us, to take Mary as his own mother. John's Gospel tells us that he took her into his own home. (Jn 19,27). This is an invitation also to us, to take Mary into our hearts and to establish with her an intimate relationship of Mother and son or daughter.

Mary's appearances in the other Gospels are infrequent but very important. We learn a great deal about her from them. When we put on the scapular, we are committing ourselves also to put on her virtues. We learn from the Gospels that she is a woman of faith, a disciple of her Son; she is humble, which means simply to know and accept the truth about oneself; she is silent, "pondering all these things in her heart". (Lk. 2,19)

She was brought up to be a good Jewess to believe that God had chosen her people to be His very own. They were to be a light to the nations and through this people was to come the messiah. There were many theories and ideas about what this messiah would do and what he would be. Like any good Jew, Our Lady would have believed that the messiah would be God's representative who would establish God's Kingdom in Israel, which would have a profound effect on the whole world.

Of course Mary was not exactly like everyone else. We have to take into account her immaculate conception. She was preserved free from all sin from the first moment of her existence. This does not of course make her less human but more human since sin is a turning away from God in whom we find the meaning of human life. To become more human means to become like Christ in whom no sin can exist. The fact that Mary was preserved free from sin means that her response to God was perfect. She held nothing back. There were no shadows; she was a fully integrated human being. The immaculate conception did not preserve her from the difficulties of being human. She had to live by faith like anyone else. What went on in the depths of her soul we can only guess at but we can catch glimpses from the picture that is built up of her in the New Testament.

At the Annunciation she is greeted as "full of grace". (Lk.1,26-38) The Lord is with her. She is afraid which is a very normal human reaction and is often the case in the Bible on the occasion of a divine manifestation. She is told not to fear. She is asked to be the mother of the messiah who will be called "Son of God". Mary had one practical question, "How can this come about as I am a virgin?" The answer she receives is that God will take care of this. The power of the Holy Spirit will overshadow her and so she will conceive. Even though it must have been difficult for her to believe and impossible to understand, she joyfully accepts the will of God and commits herself and her whole life to the unfolding of God's plan. "I am the servant of the Lord. Oh let what you have said be done to me!" (Lk. 1,38)

Because she is without sin, there is nothing in Mary that blocks the will of God. She responds perfectly. As soon as God's will is made known to her, she eagerly co-operates with the divine plan of salvation even though she does not know the details and even though she cannot comprehend what her "yes" will mean for her. She is totally at the service of God. She does not simply passively acquiesce in God's will; she eagerly and actively co-operates. She loves God and she knows from what she has been taught as well as intuitively that God loves her and that therefore the divine will is for the good of the whole people and for her too.

Mary had to walk by faith. She had to penetrate the mystery of God's plan and the mystery of her Son with loving faith. She pondered everything that happened to her and stored up everything in her heart (Lk. 2,19) in order to follow where God desired to lead her.

In the modern context, Mary shows us how to listen to the Word of God in Scripture and in life itself, how to be open to God and close to the needs of our brothers and sisters in a world where poverty in its many forms takes their dignity away. Mary further shows us the woman's path to God and stands with us as a woman who is the icon of the tenderness of God, a woman who had to face many trials in order to fulfil the vocation given to her by God.[33] She remains as the sign of freedom and liberation for all who in their oppression cry to God.[34] The Scapular on our part is an expression of our confidence in Mary's care. It shows our willingness to witness to our baptismal adoption and to being her sons and daughters, brothers and sisters, as well as our desire to be clothed with her virtues, with her contemplative spirit and with her purity of heart. Thus clothed by her, we, like her, ponder the Word and show ourselves to be disciples of her Son in our dedication to the works of God's Reign: truth and life, holiness and grace, justice, love and peace.[35]

The Word of God grew within Mary. Being a celibate male, I would not presume to suggest that I understood what goes on in the heart of a pregnant woman but I believe that it is not all joy and bliss. I suspect that the growing child within the womb can also cause various discomforts for the woman. Welcoming the Word into our lives will also demand things of us that can be uncomfortable. We will no longer be able to continue our fight with our neighbour; our unchristian attitudes and ideas will be challenged. If the Word of God is going to grow in our lives, we must repeat our consent to the presence and action of God even when this proves to be uncomfortable to us. If we are serious about the business of letting God into our lives, we will begin to experience God's presence in various ways throughout the day. By experiencing God's presence, I do not mean that we will have lovely feelings of bliss. Instead we will begin to be aware of what needs to be transformed in our lives since the presence of God will show up what is false. We will begin to become aware that we are a brother or a sister of everyone, even and

---

[33] See Paul VI, *Exhortation Marialis Cultus*, n.37

[34] Cf. John Paul II, *Redemptoris Mater*, n.37

[35] See *The Roman Missal*, Preface of the Feast of Christ the King, and Vatican II, *Constitution on the Church*, LG36. This paragraph is taken from the letter of the Superiors General of the Carmelite Orders, op. cit. no. 31

perhaps especially of those to whom we are not attracted at all. God
is love and where God is, love grows.

Welcoming the Word of God into our lives is a gradual process.
It does not happen overnight and we need to be patient with ourselves as well as with others. At the same time, we must not presume too easily that God's will has been totally accomplished in and
through us. We are on the way. Mary, our Patroness, our Mother
and our Sister, accompanies us on this long journey, which reaches
its destination in eternity.

Tradition is important not so that people can live in the past but
so that, learning from the insights of those who have gone before us
we can interpret for our own times and in our own language this
same tradition. For Carmelites, Mary has been and is the Patroness,
Mother, Sister and model of what we strive to become. The only
way in which the sincerity of any devotion can be proved is in the
way it affects daily life. Fine words are never a substitute for fine
deeds. The best devotion is to conform one's life to one's model. As
the perfect follower of Christ, she will bind us more closely to Jesus,
her Son so that we can more faithfully walk in his footsteps.

CHAPTER TWO

THE GOAL OF THE CHRISTIAN LIFE

Christ made very clear what were the conditions of following him. Those who wish to follow him must lose their lives so that they might save them. (Lk. 9,23-25) Our human ways of thinking, loving and acting, which are limited, must be transformed into divine ways, which are infinite.[36] In other words, the Christian vocation is to become like Christ, the image of the invisible God.

The goal of the spiritual journey is that we be transformed in God. The Christian vocation is to become like God, whose children we are. The Fathers of the Church spoke and wrote a great deal about the divinisation of the human being. Every aspect of the human being is to be transformed. This is normally a long, slow process, which perhaps is rarely completed in this life. To be on the spiritual journey is to be involved in this process of transformation. Relating to other human beings greatly helps this process of growth and transformation because we learn so much about ourselves, if we have eyes to see and ears to hear.

The goal of the Christian life, to put it another way, is that God's will come to fruition in each one of us and in our world. In order for this to happen, we need to be transformed and indeed the whole of creation, which is waiting with eager longing for the revelation of the children of God, must also be transformed. (Rom. 8,19)

Carmelite spirituality particularly focuses on this process of transformation in God. The Carmelite way is one way of incarnating the message of Jesus Christ.[37] All the different ways converge in Christ, who is the way, the truth and the life. (Jn. 14,6) The guiding principle of the Carmelite Rule, written by Albert, the Patriarch of Jerusalem, in the first years of the 13th century, is transformation in Christ.[38] By allowing the values of the Rule to form our lives, we will be gradually transformed so that we become a new creation in Christ. There are many ways of incarnating the Rule. There are still hermits who live it, friars, enclosed nuns, active sisters and very

---

[36] See *Constitutions of the Brothers of the Blessed Virgin Mary of Mt. Carmel*, no. 17, (Carmelite Centre, Melbourne, Australia, 1996)

[37] For an excellent overview of the Carmelite tradition and approach to spirituality, see J. Welch, *The Carmelite Way*, (Paulist Press, New York, 1996) and W. McGreal, *At the Fountain of Elijah*, (Darton, Longman & Todd, 1999).

[38] Cf. K. Waaijman, *The Mystical Space of Carmel*

many lay people, who find Carmelite spirituality an immense help in their busy lives.

We are to be transformed in God and this transformation must at least begin during our earthly existence. We are not transformed on our own but in and through our relationships with other people. Human beings need each other; that is the way we are made and it is through interaction with other human beings that we grow emotionally. How we relate on a constant basis to people and to the world around us is the test of whether we are growing in the Christian life or not.

Welcoming the Word

Our way of relating to the whole of creation must be changed radically so that each of us becomes another expression of God through our own humanity. At present our sin disfigures the presence of God in our lives. Titus Brandsma's idea is that, like Mary, we too must welcome the Word of God into our lives and pronounce our "yes".[39] This "yes" has profound effects in our lives. Imagine if you opened the door to a friend and invited that person into your home to live with you. It might be lovely for a little while to have your friend around but gradually the novelty would wear off and little things would begin to jangle your nerves. Accepting the Word of God in your life in a sense is like getting married. How long does it take for the honeymoon phase to pass? So we need to repeat our "yes" many times over. Mary said yes in the joy of the annunciation but repeated it at the foot of the cross as she watched her only Son die seemingly a failure.

Mary is the mother of the divine life in us and as our sister, she accompanies us on our journey. She is our model. We know that we must imitate the virtues of Mary but how? How can we become docile to the will of God, patient, humble and so on? To become like the Mother of God, to leave space in our lives so that God can grow in us, is the work of God. Certainly we can and must co-operate but the result of this process of transformation remains always God's work.

In what consists our co-operation? Of course we must try to live good Christian lives according to the Gospel. However those who have decided to live according to the Gospel know that this is much easier to say than to do. In the Magnificat, Mary praised and

---

[39] E. Boaga, *The Lady of the Place*, p. 90

thanked God for having accomplished great things in her. God can also do great things in us if we give God the time and space to work in us, and, above all, if we actively consent to God's presence and action in our lives. Mary was blessed not because she was the physical mother of Jesus but because she heard the Word of God and put it into practice. (Lk. 8,19-21) Mary is our model as to how we can listen to this Word and put it into practice in our own lives.

Praying the Word

Lectio Divina is the most traditional way of listening to the Word of God and of growing in an intimate relationship with God.[40] It is by means of this relationship that we are transformed and rendered capable of living the Gospel in all its fullness.

St. John of the Cross wrote, "Seek in reading and you will find in meditation. Knock in prayer and it will be opened to you in contemplation."[41] He is here outlining the traditional steps of Lectio Divina, which happily in our days is seeing a resurgence of interest. Lectio is not just a way of prayer but a way of life. I would like to use the traditional method of Lectio Divina to see how we can grow from where we are to where we want to be. The heart of Lectio Divina is the gradual growth in relationship with God. Each step of this ancient way of prayer is a step into intimacy with God.

Lectio Divina permeates the whole of the Carmelite Rule and is assumed by it. The structure of the Carmelite life is formed by this way of prayer. It was practiced for hundreds of years before any attempt was made to define it. The famous four stages or phases of Lectio Divina (reading, meditation, prayer and contemplation) come to us from the work of Guigo the Carthusian about the year 1150 in "The Ladder of the Monks".[42] Lectio Divina was lost to the vast majority of Christians especially due to fear of the influence of

---

[40] There are many books on lectio divina. An excellent study of its use in Carmel is C. Mesters, *Lectio Divina, Carmelite Spiritual Directory Project*, no. 10, (Carmelite Centre, Melbourne, Australia) 1999.

[41] *Maxims and Counsels*, 79, in the *Complete Works of St. John of the Cross*. There are two important translations: E.A. Peers, *The Complete Works of St. John of the Cross*, (Burns & Oates, London, 1954, reprinted Wheathampstead, Anthony Clarke, 1974) and K. Kavanaugh and O. Rodríguez, *The Collected Works of St. John of the Cross*, (Washington DC, ICS Publications, 1979).

[42] Translated, E. Colledge & J. Walsh, (London, Mowbray, 1978, reprint Cistercian Publications, 1981)

the Protestant principle of "Scripture Alone" and the subsequent downgrading of the importance of Tradition. Most people were denied access to the Scriptures and reading the Bible was not considered to be quite the right thing for Catholics to do. Thank God, the Word of God has once again been placed at the centre of the Church's life. Obviously it never totally disappeared and Lectio Divina was kept alive mostly within monastic settings.

The Lectio Divina method can of course be used as a method of prayer, that is one can follow the four stages in one period of prayer but Lectio Divina is a way of life rather than simply a method of prayer. The hermits on Mount Carmel allowed the Word of God to shape how they lived. They listened to the Word of God in various ways, either in the solitude of the cell or together in the chapel or in the refectory. They meditated on this Word throughout the day and spontaneously their hearts opened to God in prayer. At times all these words and thoughts were left aside in the encounter with God in silence.

A key concept to understand Lectio Divina, and indeed any way of prayer, is that of relationship.[43] We are called into an intimate relationship of friendship with God and through this relationship God will accomplish the great work of transformation in us. Let us look now at the traditional steps of the Lectio Divina process to see whether they can help us grow in intimacy with the Lord.

Reading

The first step of Lectio is to read the text of Scripture. This is our response to an initial call by Jesus Christ to follow him. We put time and effort into reading and studying the Bible, as the Word of God, and not just as an interesting ancient text. Through the pages of Scripture, God speaks directly to us. The stories of the Hebrew Bible and of the New Testament are stories also about us. All of the reading we do, whether of the Bible or of other spiritual books, must not remain only at the level of book learning; it must enter our hearts. This stage is vital for it gives us the basis from which to grow. If our reading does not enter our hearts, it remains on the surface. We need to allow the Word of God and everything else we read and learn to begin the slow process of transforming our underlying

---

[43] See E. Smith & J. Chalmers, *A Deeper Love* (Burns & Oates, U.K. & Continuum, U.S.A.), 1999, especially chapter 1

attitudes. This is the stage of gradually getting to know God, of moving slowly from learning a lot of facts about God to actually getting to know God. Of course the more deeply we come to know God, the more we accept God is Mystery and that our human words and concepts are of limited value.

Meditation

At the time the hermits were setting up their community on Mount Carmel, which would grow into a worldwide international Order, meditation was a method of memorising Scripture, especially the psalms, so that they would spontaneously come to mind throughout the day. Much later, meditation came to signify reflecting on the Scriptures or on the truths of the faith in order to raise the mind and heart to God. Over time, various strictly defined methods of meditation were introduced whereby an individual was led through a particular issue point by point in order to arrive at a dialogue with God and finally a resolution regarding his or her life. The popularity of such methods gradually waned but meditation retained its meaning of reflection on a topic in order to lead to prayer. A complicating factor in understanding the term "meditation" nowadays is the growth in interest in methods of prayer, which have their basis in Eastern religions. We have to admit that in the media and probably in the minds of most people nowadays, meditation refers to an esoteric technique of relaxation or at best a method of silent prayer.

However, in the method of Lectio Divina, meditation now normally refers to reflection on Scripture since the ancient method of repeating the words over and over in a low voice in order to fix them in the heart is very rarely mentioned in modern usage.

It is important to reflect on what we read in order to apply it to ourselves. In this way we personalise the Gospel and the great Carmelite spiritual tradition; it becomes part of us. It is quite possible to be an expert on the Bible or on Carmelite spirituality and not enter into them personally. It is possible to know a great deal about Jesus Christ but not know him at all so this stage is directed towards getting to know Jesus Christ and delving below the surface of our tradition and making it our own.

At this point of our lives, we have entered into the interior castle, which St. Teresa of Avila describes so expertly. We are not too far in at this stage but at least we have got beyond the door. There are many rooms in the castle and some are fascinating. The danger is that we will want to stay in one of them and not continue our journey to the centre where God dwells.[44] She tells us that God will not build very much without the strong foundation of humility,[45] which is to know and accept the truth about ourselves. As we continue the spiritual journey, we enter more deeply into the relationship with God. We begin to have a different perspective on things and our priorities change in view of our number one objective, which is to grow in the love and knowledge of God and to serve our brothers and sisters.

St. John of the Cross knew the tendency of the human heart to settle for much less than that for which it was created and so he wrote of the need for detachment on the journey towards total freedom, which can only be found in God. Detachment means to have a right relationship with things and people and not be enslaved by them.

At this stage, we can still be enslaved by many things and not realise it. We can be enslaved to our own opinions, the impression we want to present to others, our likes and dislikes and in many other ways. By being enslaved, I mean that, despite what we say and think, what really motivates us is not the love of God and neighbour but a less worthy motive. We may not be aware of what is driving us at this point on our journey. However, to arrive at this point, always thanks to the grace of God, we have actually become detached from many things, but we can very easily let our hearts be enslaved to other things, which are good in themselves but which are simply signs on our journey pointing us onward; they are not the goal of the journey. Therefore we can become over attached to "churchy" things, externals like the habit, vestments, incense, the "right" way of celebrating the liturgy and so on. They are intended to help us and they are undoubtedly important but they are not the be-all and end-all of existence. They are pointers on our journey but they cannot give us what our hearts crave. We must continue the journey.

The human heart is very subtle and tends to become enslaved in very subtle ways. St. Teresa of Avila describes the person who has

---

[44] *Interior Castle* in the *Complete Works of St. Teresa of Avila*. There are two important English translations. The earlier is that of E.A. Peers, *Complete Works of St. Teresa*, (London, Sheed & Ward, 1957). The later is by K. Kavanaugh & O. Rodriguez, *The Collected Works of St. Teresa of Avila*, Washington DC, ICS Publications, 1976).

[45] See for example what St. Teresa has to say about the importance of humility as the foundation of a life of prayer: *Life* 10,5; 12,4; 22,11

reached the third mansions of the interior castle as a very good person. The trouble is that the person's religion is too well ordered. He or she needs to move beyond this point. The problem is not in the practice or the thing but in our hearts. What are we seeking? Does this external reality give us what we are looking for – security, self-esteem, control of our own little world?

The Word of God is alive and active. It is our story and speaks directly to our lives. We gradually become more and more interested in the Person who is the protagonist of the Bible – God. A desire is awoken within us for a personal encounter with God. At this point the heart comes into play and we begin to search for God. This searching can be painful and can take a long time. Sometimes God seems to hide from us just at the point where we have begun to seek Him. As St. John of the Cross says:-

Where hast thou hidden thyself
And has left me, Beloved to my sighing?
Thou didst flee like the hart, having wounded me:
I went out after thee calling, and thou wert gone." [46]

At this point we can give up the search because it is too difficult but we would have lost the greatest treasure of our lives, or we can continue to seek God wherever that may lead us.

Hopefully the meditation gradually becomes prayer where we in some way encounter the One who calls us. Our hearts become captivated. The message reaches our hearts and becomes really meaningful and relevant to our daily reality. We are gradually drawn towards God as Person and not just the message.

It is a very common experience for those who reflect on the Word of God on a regular basis that what once gave them so much satisfaction gradually fails to satisfy. Many seem to give up meditation, in the sense of reflection, because they do not find it useful any more. Perhaps we found it helpful for a while but then it no longer gave us anything, so we did not continue with it. This is a critical moment on the spiritual journey. St. Teresa of Avila reminds us that in the matter of prayer, we need a very determined determination to continue and never give up no matter what the obstacles may be.[47] Perhaps we gave up meditation because we became lukewarm. If that is the case, we need have no fear of returning, as God is always

---

[46] *Spiritual Canticle*, Stanza 1
[47] *Way of Perfection* 21,2

eager to listen to us and to speak to our hearts. We need to read the Word of God and ponder on it in order to apply it to our own lives.

Perhaps, however, we gave up meditation because it became boring and we felt there was no point in sitting day after day bored out of our minds when we could be doing something useful like visiting the sick, or writing letters, or reading the paper or watching the television! Prayer is an intimate conversation with the One whom we know loves us.[48] Prayer is wasting time with God. It is most certainly not a waste of time but it is time we freely give to God when we could be doing other things. If we are not willing to waste time with a friend, no friendship exists. Conversation is a two-way affair. Some people seem to have great difficulty listening to others. They love to hear the sound of their own voice and what the other says does not seem to penetrate. God often waits until we are ready to hear. Sometimes we receive a wake-up call. These calls will become more insistent as time goes on but our ability to interpret them will lessen as we become less used to listening to the voice of God. So, if we find listening particularly difficult, we need to make a very special effort. God is never outdone in generosity. Any effort we make will be repaid a hundred-fold.

The reason for our boredom at prayer might not be lukewarmness or an inability to listen. It might be a call from God to move on to another way of relating. This is where we move from friendliness into friendship. As we grow in a human relationship, we often encounter difficulties that test our friendship. There is a charming story about St. Teresa of Avila, which points out that we should not expect our relationship with God always to run smoothly. It is said that she was out in atrocious weather on one of her many journeys. At a certain point her carriage became stuck in deep mud. She pointed out to the Lord that if he treated friends in that fashion, it was no wonder he had so few of them!

If we are going to become close friends with anyone, we must learn to accept that person as he or she is. If we wish to accept the invitation to be intimate friends of Jesus Christ, we must accept the disconcerting ways he works.

Prayer

Prayer is an essential aspect of our lives. God initiates the dialogue and prayer is our response; through prayer we deepen the

---

[48] Cf. St. Teresa, *Life* 8,5

relationship with God in Christ. There is an external aspect to prayer, which is important but is not the only aspect. The externals are intended to help us penetrate deeper. Just as in a progressively deepening human relationship, the ways of communicating with God become less complicated. At this stage the impact of God in our lives becomes more profound.

There is usually some sort of crisis that occurs in a relationship that calls forth a fundamental decision whether to continue with the relationship and therefore get into deeper water or to "cool it". Unlike a normal human relationship, Christ continually pursues us whether we want to deepen the relationship or not. It is quite possible to go through life dipping a toe into the ocean but never taking the plunge. Taking the plunge in the relationship with God means making a real commitment to God. This commitment need not be of a public nature but must have a real effect on the way we live and relate to others.

If we do seek to grow in our relationship with God, spontaneous prayer often seems to give way to silence where we allow the Spirit of God to pray within us. Scripture says, "The Spirit too comes to help us in our weakness. For when we cannot choose words in order to pray properly, the Spirit expresses our plea in a way that could never be put into words, and God who knows everything in our hearts, knows perfectly well what he means ...." (Rom. 8,26-27).

When our prayer becomes silence, it may appear to us that we are wasting time. The temptation is to return to a form of prayer where we were in control and when at least we had the sense of doing something, when we had the satisfaction that we were indeed praying. However silence is a perfectly normal development of prayer. There comes a time when all our words need to be laid aside because they cannot express what is in our hearts. In silence God can hear what is in our hearts and in silence, we can hear the still small voice of God. We can parallel this experience with the normal development of a friendship where two people become more and more comfortable with each other without the use of many words.

Contemplation

Contemplation is the goal of Lectio Divina and indeed of all prayer. In Chapter Four, I will examine the idea of contemplation more deeply but for the moment, I just want to say that it cannot be confined to an experience or set of experiences no matter how exalted or refined. Contemplation is the relationship with God that has reached maturity. John of the Cross and Teresa mostly describe this in terms of prayer but are at pains to point out that contemplation has a profound effect on daily life. Prayer is the irreplaceable door into contemplation but there is much more to contemplation than the specific time we set aside for formal prayer. A contemplative is one who is praying constantly, in the sense of being in tune with the will of God and who at every moment carries out God's will. In this sense a contemplative is one who prays constantly because he or she is in constant touch with God, whether on a conscious level or not.

The intimate encounter with God fulfils the yearnings of our hearts. At this point thoughts, images, words, perceptions, meditation, petitions and so on become rather unnecessary and even not fully meaningful or helpful. We simply rest in God and we have a simple loving awareness of God's presence. The more we rest in God, the deeper God can work in us as we are slowly shaped to become what God knows we can be - images of Christ. At this point reading the Scriptures has become food for life and not just food for thought.

These four stages of Lectio Divina- reading, meditating, prayer and contemplation are like Jacob's ladder. We go up and down constantly even in one period of prayer. The reading and meditating prepares the way for prayer, which in turn prepares us for contemplation. All prayer is a grace from God but this refers in a particular way to contemplation. The first two stages can also be present throughout the day as we read the Scriptures at different times and think about what we have read so that at the times we have set aside to simply be with God, we can, with little immediate preparation, begin to pray. Prayer as the personal encounter with God lays the way open to contemplation.

To pray at all in the broad sense means to enter into relationship with God. God's work in us is to bring us to our human fulfilment where we show forth the image of Christ in which we were created. However we cover over our real selves, made in the image and likeness of God with a shell. We have various masks with which we present ourselves to the world outside. Gradually we must allow God to gently remove this shell and these masks one by one so that we stand before God as we really are. God knows what we are already but we do not, so prayer, as well as being an encounter with God, is also an encounter with ourselves.

To arrive at this point is not the end of the journey but the beginning of another phase of the spiritual journey. One is not perfect at this stage but mature. There are still many areas for growth in the future.

Growing in Love

In order to understand the spiritual journey better, it may be useful to connect it to our ordinary human experience. Human beings
have been made for love and in order for us to grow, relationships
are necessary. However there are many difficulties involved in
developing relationships. Our natural tendency is to seek to avoid
difficulties but if we do that we run the risk of shallowness in all our
relationships, which means that we may grow in years but not in
human maturity.

We can outline four basic stages in the development of human
relationships. First of all there is the stage of first meeting. Here we
begin to get to know the person and we show an interest. Hopefully this is reciprocated. If not, no real relationship will develop.
Then follows the stage of making the acquaintance of the other. We
want to spend time with that person. What we have learned about
the other whets our appetite for more and so we begin to exchange
ideas, opinions and our concerns. Gradually a friendship may
develop and a friendship exists where there is a certain level of intimacy, affection and self-disclosure. In order for this to take place,
there must be a growing trust between the parties. However friendship makes us vulnerable to being hurt and no one likes to be hurt.
There is a danger at this point of backing off and withdrawing into
our shell for fear of the possible hurt. Real friendship can be very
demanding. It demands a personal commitment to the other person
and some people do not want demands made on them, but without
friendship in our lives, we will be stunted human beings.

As the friendship grows and develops, love grows between the
two parties. Romantic love is only one example of love and love
must not be reduced to this. When we love another, we can simply
be with that person, without saying anything.

These four steps in human relationships find a parallel in the
four steps of Lectio Divina.[49]   When we read the Word of God, we
get to know God a little. We listen with respectfulness and we are
receptive to what God wants to say to us. The second stage, which
is the level of acquaintanceship is paralleled in the stage of meditation where, desiring to spend more time with the person, we begin
to share interests. We reflect and ponder on God's word and we seek
to apply it to our daily lives. Gradually we grow in friendship with

---

[49] This point in developed further in E. Smith & J. Chalmers, *A Deeper Love*,
chapters 1 & 2

God and meditation gives way to a spontaneous prayer arising from our hearts. There is then an affective response to God's initiative and we begin to long to be in God's presence. Gradually there develops a greater transparency as we get to know God better and we allow ourselves to be known. When true love grows, we are content to simply rest in the mystery of God.

The Christian life is not just a matter of will power but of allowing the power of Christ to work within us and to transform us. The very early saints and great figures of the Church often preached and wrote about what they called the "divinisation" of the human being. They said that God became human so that men and women could become God and by this they meant that the Christian vocation is to respond wholeheartedly to God's invitation to new life and in this way become like God.

So the goal of the Christian life is to become like God. However, we know from the story of the Fall in the book of Genesis that this is not something which human beings can grasp for themselves; it is a free gift of grace in Jesus Christ. Our part is to respond to the invitation to enter into an intimate relationship of friendship with God and we do so in a variety of ways. Obviously we try to live as God wants us to, according to the message of Christ. However, Christianity is not principally about what we do but about what God does in us. An essential element for a renewal of Christian life is prayer, understood as a relationship with God. Any relationship takes time to develop and grow. Each human being is a mystery and we never plumb the depths of another person. So, the relationship with God is even more mysterious. Entering into the relationship with God is to embark on a never-ending journey.

The Scriptures use many analogies for God's relationship with the chosen people but perhaps the closest is the bond of marriage. God wants to be united with us. People fall in love and this perhaps blinds them to the nature of the commitment they are making in marriage. However when the honeymoon phase ends, will the couple continue to grow in their mutual commitment? Falling in love is easy but truly loving is not at all easy; it is the most difficult thing we can do but at the same time it is the most rewarding. As Christians we are to love one another and by this, and in no other way, will we be known as disciples of Christ. We will not be known as Christ's disciples by how many degrees we have, or how busy we are or how many prayers we say. The test is - can we love or not?[50] Love

---

[50] See St. John of the Cross: "In the evening we will be judged in love" in Sayings of Light and Love, 57

comes from God and only if we are united with Christ as the branches are united with the vine, can we love.

Love is a total commitment, a total self-surrender. Obviously it is
not just having lovely feelings. We are naturally afraid to surrender
ourselves totally into the hands of God because deep down we
realise that God is ultimately unknowable and we do not want to
lose ourselves totally. At first then God usually attracts us very gently and invites us to go deeper. God calls and we respond; if I decide
to keep God at the level of an acquaintance, God will not force me
to go deeper, although the invitations will not cease. You cannot
force someone to be your friend. It is sad to see people being more
than satisfied with a very superficial relationship with God. We
grow only insofar as we allow God into our lives and it would appear
that many people do not want to grow. Growing is a painful process
with many tears but to avoid the agony is to miss the ecstasy. As we
grow, we leave behind previous stages and this is a form of dying.
We must let go the past in order to receive the present.

In our relationship with God when the honeymoon phase ends,
we enter a critical moment. Are we prepared to be faithful to God
even when it is boring and unattractive? Most people who pray will
enter what John of the Cross calls the night of sense after a fairly
brief time.[51] The dark night is not something to be frightened about;
it is a normal stage of growth and usually happens in and through
the events of daily life. Some people, however, seem to always want
God to do their bidding and when they begin to discover that God is
not as they first imagined, they are not quite so eager to get
involved. Usually such people will not abandon prayer altogether;
they will continue to say some prayers and they will be "good" people who are quite satisfied with themselves but they will have
stopped growing. They will still love but not too much; they will
have settled for comfortable mediocrity.

The Pharisees are a salutary example for us. They were not at all
bad men; they were good men, obedient to the law of God. They
searched the Scriptures, gave alms to the poor and prayed on a regular basis. Yet they are the ones who are condemned by Jesus, not the
public sinners. They had substituted human rules and regulations for
the will of God. They refused to recognise in Jesus the one of whom
the Scriptures spoke and therefore they refused to go to him for life

---

[51] *The Dark Night*, I,8,4.

because as Jesus himself said, "you cannot bear to hear my word" (Jn.8,43).

To reduce religion to rules and regulations is a tragedy; it is a relationship with the Living God. But to encounter the God of Abraham, of Isaac, of Jacob, the Father of Jesus is an earth-shaking event. At first God may approach us very gently through part of creation but there will be a time when we must come face to face with the awesomeness of the Living God. In that encounter all our self-deception and illusions are swept away from us. But my self-deception is comfortable; I do not want to stand naked before God. "The man and his wife heard the sound of the Lord God walking in the garden in the cool of the day, and they hid from the Lord God among the trees of the garden. But the Lord God called to the man, 'Where are you?' he asked. 'I heard the sound of you in the garden;' he replied. 'I was afraid because I was naked so I hid." (Gen. 3, 8-10)

Usually there will be a gradual process whereby God helps us to let go control. We must learn that we cannot control God like the hot water tap and so our experience of prayer may be dry from time to time. The initial stages of this process are often marked by unpredictability. The dryness comes and goes and we never know whether our prayer time is going to be dry as dust or a really good experience. Letting go control is not at all an easy matter. It is one thing to say that we abandon ourselves to God and quite another to live this abandonment out in practice. There are so many subtle ways we have of deceiving ourselves. We can filter everything and so we only hear what we want to hear. I may not "hear" a sermon, which calls me to repent; I can search the Scriptures like the Pharisees but not be open to the Word of God. I can refuse to accept God's Word because it does not come to me in the expected package or from an acceptable person. The spiritual journey requires tremendous honesty but our honesty produces a reward beyond anything that we could conceive of.

There are very many good, sincere people but how many are prepared to pay the price of complete self-surrender to God? We know that we can do nothing without grace but we seem quite prepared to construct our own way to God, our own path to holiness. Yet this is impossible. God knows what we were created to be and only by allowing God full freedom in our lives can we arrive at our destination, which involves us in a total transformation.

The goal of the Christian life is totally impossible for human beings to achieve. For this we need a desire to trust God without limit. If we are to be transformed in God, we must let go of everything. At the beginning we can be so attracted by God that letting go of gross sin is not too difficult. But then we must let go of our desire to control our own life, other people's lives and even our desire to control God.

If we really desire God and try to co-operate with God's will and are not just playing at being spiritual, I believe that there will come a time when God will really respond to our desires. God will do so by removing any rivals for the centre spot. We may sincerely believe that there are no rivals to God in our lives. Can I trust God, radically trust God when what I hold most dear is cut away and removed? What I am called to let go of at this crucial time is any disordered attachment, which remains in my life. A disordered attachment is a relationship or connection to any person, place or thing from which I am seeking total satisfaction or which enslaves my heart.[52] The problem is that by this stage I think that I have let go of everything I consider to be a disordered attachment and only healthy ones remain! However God thinks differently.

St. John of the Cross wrote that it matters little whether a bird is tied down by a stout cord or a slender thread.[53] It depends on what the bird wants to do. If all it desires is to scrabble in the dirt round about it, then being tied does not matter. However if it wants to fly, the cord or thread must be cut. The problem is that at this time we may only be tied by a thread but we may consider that the thread is not tying us down at all but is in fact pulling us up to God, i.e. we may consider the thread to be a very good thing to which we are quite rightly attached. There is still a very subtle struggle for control.

Very subtly I want God to conform to my ways of thinking. Do I try to mould God to fit what I think God should will or am I really and truly open to have my mind and my little world expanded immensely?

There are some obvious disordered attachments and the self-love contained in them is equally obvious but at certain points things can get quite subtle because my search for self-gratification is camouflaged by my desire for God's glory.

When we pray we are relating to God. If we cannot relate to people then I think that we are going to have a few difficulties relating to God because the relationship with God follows a similar pattern to other relationships. For a relationship to grow, trust has got to be

---

[52] See J. Welch, *When Gods Die*, (New York, Paulist Press, 1990) for an excellent explanation of this phenomenon.

[53] *The Ascent of Mount Carmel, I,* 11,4

built up. We build trust by spending time with the other, sharing concerns, hopes, dreams and so on. We cannot jump too quickly into intimacy.

God courts us and continually invites us deeper into the Mystery. It is only within God that we shall find the answer to our own mystery. Prayer begins with God's invitation to us that comes in all sorts of different ways. God is ever inventive. If you want to meet a particular person, it is a good idea to go to a place where you know he or she will be. God comes to where we are whether that is a good place or not. God calls us from that place and invites us to begin a journey. If we refuse, God waits and reissues the invitation in a different way. God never gives up. When we do respond, God gently leads us along into a relationship of intimacy.

It is very natural that at the beginning of a deepening relationship with God we will use many words. We have to get to know God and we have so much to say. Some people lose interest when they discover that God does not respond exactly they way they want. Others learn and accept that God's ways are not our ways. They learn to follow where God leads. Gradually the torrent of words slows down and we are able to simply be with God without too many words. Listening begins to become an important part of our prayer. We focus on the Word rather than on many words.   When we begin to quieten down, we become aware of the under-current of noise within us. This noise is almost always present and we have become so used to it that we often do not notice it. It is only when we enter silence that the internal noise comes to the surface of our consciousness. Silence is of course not just a lack of words. It is a way of communicating. Indeed silence is God's way of communicating par excellence. As St. John of the Cross wrote, "The Father spoke one Word which was His Son and He speaks it in an eternal silence, and in silence it must be heard by the soul." [54]

---

[54] *Maxims and Counsels*, 21

CHAPTER THREE

HEARING THE WORD

In order for us to hear the Word of God, we obviously must listen to it. However, that is easier said than done. Listening is an art that is not easy to learn. We have very subtle ways to avoid hearing what we do not want to hear. Listening is one of the most difficult skills to learn. One day I was told by an expert in counselling that the most important thing about being a counsellor was the ability to listen. I would have agreed if I could have got a word in edgeways but he had me pinned down for an hour and a half and I do not think that he took a breath between words! How true are the words of Robert Burns, the national poet of Scotland:
"O wad some pow'r the Giftie gie us
 To see oursels as others see us.
 It wad from monie a blunder free us
 An' foolish notion."[55]

I will translate for those unfortunate enough not to have studied the poetry of Burns! "If only God would give us the gift of being able to see ourselves as other people see us! It would save us from many a blunder and foolish notion".

It is not easy to see ourselves or to know ourselves. John of the Cross describes beginners in his work, "The Dark Night".[56] He paints a devastating picture of these good people who still have a long way to go on the spiritual journey. He does so in order that people will understand that union with God involves us in a total transformation of our being and that God alone can bring this about. Our role is to co-operate with God's grace.

We begin the journey of transformation when we hear God's call to take the relationship with God seriously and begin to do something about it. There may very well have been many years of preparation for the journey when we have tried and failed, sometimes countless times, to satisfy the deep hungers of our heart. Perhaps we have received several "wake up" calls throughout our life, i.e.

---

[55] Robert Burns, *To a Louse*. Burns was inspired to write this little speech to a flea, which he spotted crawling on the large hat of a very haughty young woman. He happened to be sitting behind the young lady in church and obviously became a little distracted. There are many editions of Burns' poetry. The one I have to hand is Penguin Books, edited by W. Beattie and H. Meikle, U.K., 1972

[56] *Book I*, 1-7

events which try to shake us out of our complacency so that we will respond wholeheartedly to what God is asking of us.

What happens when we really do decide to take God seriously? St. Teresa of Avila, in her famous example, pictures the human being as a castle made up of many rooms. She says that the door of the castle is prayer and she warns that many people never even get through the door. The first rooms of this castle are called the rooms of self-knowledge.[57] Indeed self-knowledge must be our constant companion throughout the whole spiritual journey. Self-knowledge is not easy and we can cling to comfortable self-delusion.   Our vocation is to be transformed by God so that we become like God, seeing as if with God's eyes and loving as if with God's heart. The truth is that we are far from that ideal and that we have a long road to travel. One of the most difficult lessons to really learn is that this is God's work and that we cannot save ourselves. This might seem to be obvious and we can easily think that we have learned that lesson a long time ago but little things will give us away. Do we really trust in God or do we say that we trust in God but have little "insurance policies" dotted throughout our lives by which we try to save ourselves? Our job is to prepare the ground and keep it fertile so that the seed of eternal life might blossom and that we might become all that God has planned for us.

Listening in the Gospels

We need to listen to God's Word and hear it so that it will have a transforming effect on our lives. Let us look at some biblical examples of how difficult it is to really hear what God is saying to us.

The Gospels are full of incidents that manifest the complete lack of understanding of the apostles and others regarding what Jesus was trying to accomplish. It is easy to accept that the enemies of Jesus did not understand him but what about his closest friends? One powerful pointer to the truth of the Gospels is that they are not afraid to show how slow the apostles were to understand what Jesus was talking about. They were the pillars of the church and the faith of many was based on their preaching and yet they found great difficulty in really hearing Jesus.

Why do the Gospels make the point so repeatedly that the disciples failed to understand Jesus' message? I believe that this point is

---

[57] *Interior Castle*, I, 1-2

made so forcefully because of the great danger of the readers making the same mistake. We can and do filter the message of Jesus through our own preconceived notions. We can adapt the message of Jesus to our own agenda. Therefore the Gospel can be turned into a thing and manipulated. There are very many examples of this throughout history.

Jesus called Simon to be one of his first followers and gave him a new name, Peter, the rock. Peter saw many miracles, including the cure of his own mother-in-law. Despite everything that he saw and heard, Peter's faith seems to have been very weak at the beginning of his time with Jesus. When he was in the boat and the storm arose, he, along with the other disciples, was mortally afraid. Jesus was asleep and the disciples woke him up. He calmed the storm but rebuked them for their lack of faith. On another occasion, in response to Jesus' request, Peter and the others put out their nets despite having toiled all night with no result. They were rewarded with a huge catch that nearly broke their nets. As a result of this miraculous catch, Peter recognised his sinfulness and the gulf between himself and Jesus, at least at a certain level. However he had to learn a lot more about himself. The closer we allow God to come to us, the more clearly do we see ourselves. This can be very painful but is in fact a healing process. We tend to have many illusions about ourselves. If we spend time with Jesus, our illusions will begin to fall away and we come face to face with ourselves as we really are.

Peter was convinced that Jesus was the promised messiah and he was excited. I wonder whether he really heard what Jesus said about the conditions of discipleship. Did he really understand Jesus' message? When Jesus asked the disciples who the people thought he might be, they were full of things to say. Then Jesus made it more personal. He asked them all, "And you, who do you say that I am?" (Mt. 16, 15). Peter broke the silence and spoke up for all of them. He made his profession of faith that Jesus was the messiah. Jesus told Peter how happy and blessed he was; he was the rock on which the Church would be built. Just imagine how Peter must have felt at this point. Imagine being praised like this by Jesus and in front of so many companions! Then Jesus began to tell his disciples that he would soon be rejected, suffer terribly, be killed but that he would rise again on the third day. Peter clearly knew a little bit about life and so he took Jesus aside to point out the error of his ways. What Jesus then said must have stung Peter terribly, "Get behind me, satan. You are an obstacle in my path, because the way you think is not God's way but man's". (Mt. 16, 23).

The darkness that Peter must have experienced at that moment was a healing darkness. Through it he learned to grow. He was challenged to radically change his outlook from ordinary human ways of thinking to God's ways. We are told through the Prophet Isaiah that God's ways and thoughts are not our ways and thoughts (Is. 55,8). When Peter and the other disciples were called by Jesus, they were fascinated by him. He healed the sick and proclaimed a message of good news and hope. They came to believe that he was the messiah but they assumed that he would act according to the accepted ways of thinking.

We have a wonderful facility for blocking out what we do not want to hear. How often have we read the Gospel and heard it proclaimed but have we really grasped what God is saying to us? We tend to have worked out our own ideas of God and a way of living that is generally quite comfortable and we do not want anything to disturb our equilibrium. Therefore we listen to the Word of God but we tend to hear only what we want to hear. Peter was challenged to change his whole way of thinking and acting in a radical fashion. He was challenged to allow God to be God and not try to limit the divine to human ways of thinking.

God is much greater than our limited and limiting vision. Peter expected Jesus to follow his way of thinking. The revolution in Peter's thinking did not happen overnight. He had to go through many experiences and shocks. We are told that the apostles were out in their boat but Jesus had not gone with them. Then he came towards them, in the middle of the night, walking on the water! They were frightened because they thought it was a ghost. People do not walk on water. It is impossible and so it must have been some sort of ghostly apparition. However, this ghostly being called out to them in their fear, "Courage, it's me! Don't be afraid!" It looked a bit like Jesus and it sounded like him but of course it could not be him. Despite all the miracles they had seen, the faith of the apostles was still weak.

Peter was a little bit bolder than the rest and so he tested this apparition. He said, "Lord, if it is you, tell me to come to you across the water." (Mt. 14,28). Jesus answered very simply, "Come". Credit must be given to Peter; he gave it a go. He actually began to walk on the water. It was impossible but he was doing it. As soon as he realised what he was doing, he took fright and then he plunged beneath the waves. He became aware that what he was doing was impossible and then he began to sink. He cried out to Jesus to save him and Jesus grasped hold of him and brought him safely back to the boat. Jesus said to Peter, "Man of little faith, why did you doubt?" We can too easily limit God to our own ways of thinking and acting.

Then Jesus took Peter, James and John up the mountain where he was transfigured before their eyes. Moses and Elijah appeared to them and God even spoke to them in the cloud, telling them to listen to Jesus, the Beloved of the Father. (Mt. 17,1-8). This wonderful experience was to prepare them for the dreadful experience of the Passion. Even after all this, Peter along with the other disciples, could be found arguing about who would be the greatest in the Kingdom of God. Had they understood nothing? Peter must have been full of enthusiasm at the beginning when he was first called to follow Jesus. There was a brief period of success but then crisis followed. Most people did not accept Jesus and his message was largely ignored. The religious leaders vehemently rejected him. This was first of all a crisis for Jesus himself. He had to come to terms with the fact that the road he was travelling would lead inexorably to the cross. This had to be introduced very gradually to the apostles, and even so it came as a terrible shock to them.

Nothing could really prepare Peter and the others for the horror of the Passion. At the Last Supper, Jesus warned Peter that Satan had been granted his wish to sift all the disciples like wheat. There is a moment of testing that comes to us all. Is our faith deeply rooted? Are our outward signs of religion an overflowing of what is in the heart or are they only external? Perhaps the testing and sifting will show us that there is a great deal more superficiality in us than we ever thought. Even at the stage of the Last Supper, Peter did not know himself. He said to Jesus, "Even though I have to die with you, I will never disown you." (Mt. 26,35). This is obviously a man who really loves Jesus. Peter does not completely understand Christ's mission but yet he has accepted that the way of the messiah may not be all glory. Words however are cheap. Only action can prove the truth of the words we use.

God does not want us to see our failures in order to depress us but to make us aware to the very depths of our being that without God we can do nothing but with God all things are possible. In response to Peter's avowal that he would be prepared to die with Christ, Jesus gently points out that very shortly Peter will deny him. In the Garden of Gethsemane when Jesus needed him most, he was asleep, and then during the trial when Jesus needed a friend, Peter deserted him and denied even knowing him.

After Jesus had risen from the dead, he appeared to Peter and forgave him. He gave Peter the mission of feeding his lambs and sheep.

Peter went on to strengthen the other disciples and preach the Gospel everywhere.

The experience of Peter was a long learning process of what it really meant to follow Jesus. He had to learn by his own experience of failure and in the darkness there came light. At the beginning Jesus saw something in Simon that caused Jesus to call him Peter, "the Rock". Simon became Peter because he grew to become what Jesus knew he could be through all the ups and downs of his life.

The greatest danger to our growth is to believe that we have no more to learn or no more growing to do. If we think that we already are everything we can be, then we are not open to further growth. The Word of God is addressed to us in many different ways each day. God gradually reveals to us what we are if we are open to hearing the Word and often this revelation will come in moments of darkness and through those areas of our lives, which we would rather not look at. This revelation is for our growth. God can see what is in us and what our possibilities are. God knows that we can be far more that we are now.

When Jesus first called Simon the Rock, the name did not seem to reflect reality. In much of the Gospel, Peter does not seem to be much of a rock. Perhaps a better definition of him would be "a jelly". He seemed to be rather unstable, impulsive, rushing in without understanding the situation, making rash promises and then failing to deliver. Despite all the miracles he had seen, he still had great difficulty in believing that the power of God was in Jesus. He had limited God to his own way of thinking. Yet Simon did indeed become the rock on which the faith of the Church is built. Jesus saw all the possibilities in him and drew them out of him.

Remember what happened to Jesus when he went to his hometown. At first the people were astonished at his wisdom. Was there a chance that they could actually accept the Word of God in an unfamiliar garb? But then the shutters came down very quickly. "This is the carpenter's son, surely? Is not his mother the woman called Mary, and his brothers James and Joseph and Simon and Jude? His sisters too are they not here with us? So where did he get it all? And they would not accept him." (Mt. 13,54-58). It is difficult to hear the Word of God because we do not want to have to change.

Imagine if God had approached other young women before Our Lady. Imagine a very good and pious young woman; she is at prayer and she really wants to do God's will. This young woman has one or two blocks, which she does not recognise. Anyway while she is at prayer, the angel of the Lord appears to her and says, "The Lord is

with you." She was deeply disturbed by these words and asked herself what this greeting could mean, but the angel said to her, "do not
be afraid, you have won God's favour. Listen." At this the young
woman replied, "wait a minute, you're not the angel of the Lord.
Angels have six wings; you only have two. You cannot be from God.
I am not going to listen to you." And the angel said to her, "but not
all angels have six wings; some only need two. Anyway it is not the
wings that count." But the young woman said, "of course angels
have six wings. It quite clearly says so in Isaiah chapter 6 verse 2 and
anyway my mother told me so. Go away." The angel said, "but you
haven't even heard my message. You will be missing the greatest
blessing of your life if you send me away now. You will be refusing
to do God's will." At this the young woman got quite angry but
because she was so good, she always remained in control so she did
not show her anger but, gathering up all her offended dignity, she
said very calmly and firmly, "I have always tried to do God's will; I
have always tried to follow the inspiration of God's Spirit. Now go
away..." And the angel left her.

Do we not do something similar from time to time? Do we not
reject God's angels because we do not like the way they dress or look
or their tone of voice? Do we not reject the Word of God sometimes
because we do not like the package?

The human condition

There is something not quite right with the human condition.
The biblical writers called it the Fall and attributed all the problems
in the world to human sin. Whatever the reason, there is certainly
something wrong. Something always seems to spoil even our best
intentions. We are born with certain natural instincts, which, over
the course of the years, tend to form into voracious demands. For
example we are born with a need to be loved and cared for. This
very easily turns into a demand that everyone dance attention on us
and respond promptly to our every whim. There is a selfish streak
in every human being and, left unchecked, this will take over our
lives. All these different demands as well as the conditioning we
receive within our own culture, go to form the false self.[58] There are
various ways of describing and explaining the false self. I just want

---

[58] See T. Keating, *Invitation to Love*, (Element, Massachusetts & Dorset), Chaps.
1-4 and E. Smith and J. Chalmers, *A Deeper Love*, Chapter 8 for a fuller description
of the false self.

to say very simply that the false self is the way we try to save ourselves instead of allowing God to save us.

Relating to other people can help us become mature friends of
Jesus Christ. It does help immensely if we are willing to accept what
we learn about ourselves through our interaction with others. We
will find that we are not actually very patient and tolerant after all.
We will discover anger that we did not know we possessed. Relating to other people brings out the false self. The phenomenon of
someone who is regarded as very holy by outsiders but the opposite
by those who have to live with the particular individual is easily
understood when we look at it from the perspective of the false self.
With outsiders, one can maintain a distance and the false self will
not be so easily spotted, but living in close proximity to others
means that our negative traits become obvious very quickly.

Our relationships will teach us a great deal about ourselves if we
are willing to listen. It is a great temptation, however, to blame others for our problems. We often project our own problems onto others. We can escape the searching questions that are posed to us by
simply opting out of close relationships. Our emotions will inform
us of what truly motivates us. If we are angry with someone or with
a group, it is possible that our anger is fully justified, but it is very
likely that the source is some interior unresolved issue. The false
self is searching for infinite amounts of esteem, security and control
and when these needs are not met, it will not be happy at all. Just
because we say a few prayers now and again and read a bit of Scripture, does not mean that our false self is dead. Far from it! The
death of the false self, I believe, is what Jesus is speaking of in the
Gospel when he tells us that those who seek to save their lives will
lose them and only those who are prepared to lose their lives for him
and for the sake of the Gospel, will save them. (cf. Lk. 9, 24) The
whole spiritual journey is a struggle with the false self so that we can
be finally transformed in Christ. I do not think that we should claim
to be transformed too quickly.

Beginners, according to John of the Cross, really think they are
something. People who have advanced on the journey learn humility, which means knowing and accepting the truth about themselves.
We gradually learn what motivates us if we are willing to listen to
our hearts. Perhaps the real reason for some of the difficulties we
have with other people is that we are angry, not necessarily with
anyone in particular, but at life in general because of the hand we
have been dealt. Perhaps the reason for the lack of prayer in our
life is that we are afraid to face God because we know we will have

to let go of something that is important to us. Perhaps the motive for our tireless work is that we do not want to stop and think. So the initial stages of the dark night are painful because we have to face ourselves at a certain level. If we had thought that we were God's gift to the Church or the world, this revelation can come as something of a shock. When we begin to accept these painful facts about ourselves, we are on the way to purity of heart. Perhaps we will never arrive there in this life but it is better to be on the journey than not to have begun at all.

In order to listen seriously to the Word of God, our receptive faculties must be enlarged and purified. We can and must do our best but in the end only God can bring our work to completion. Our capacity for listening is limited by the filter which each of us has within us. This filter is formed by our motives, some of which we are not even aware. For example, if I do not believe that I have any need for repentance, I will not hear the appeal of the Gospel to conversion. At least this appeal will not penetrate into my inmost being and therefore no transformation will take place in my life. I am not thinking about a first conversion from a life far from God, but rather I am referring to a second phase of conversion in which we abandon ourselves into the hands of God so that God can accomplish the work of transformation in us. St. John of the Cross and St. Teresa of Avila both write of a stage on the spiritual journey which is good but at the same time dangerous. John describes the state of beginners who believe themselves to be much better than they in fact are. St. Teresa, in the Interior Castle, places these people in the 3rd mansions describing them as good Christians but whose lives are guided by good sense and who still lack an ardent love and who must be transformed in God.

We are born into a fallen world. As we come into the world, we take on the human condition which means that we experience ourselves as separated from God, who is the source of all being, and outside of whom the human heart can have no lasting happiness. The spiritual journey is the return to our Source. Indeed our hearts are restless until they find their rest in God. At birth we are of course not fully formed and the ability to use reason only comes slowly. A baby is helpless and so is in need of love, of feeling secure and of having his or her basic needs met. The human heart, even in the little body of a baby, is a vast cavern. The human heart is made for God and only God can fully and finally satisfy it. A baby's needs for love, for security, and for survival are infinite and no parents, no matter how wonderful, can completely satisfy these needs. As a child grows up, he or she begins to compensate for what is felt to be missing. Objectively a child may appear to have everything but it is the subjective experience that is important. If I do not <u>feel</u> loved, <u>feel</u> secure, <u>feel</u> some control of my environment, whatever the reality might be, I will find ways of compensating for what I feel is lacking. Very quickly the child develops little ways of seeking affection, of gaining control of his or her life and of making sure that he or she survives in all circumstances. These, the child "believes" at a deep level will bring happiness.

With the onset of reason, this faculty is used to support the individual's ways of gaining happiness. The family and cultural background also support these compensatory methods, e.g. if "my Dad is bigger than your Dad", or if "my school is better than your school" or if "my country is better than your country" or if "my Order is bigger than your Order", or if "my religion is better than your religion", I will feel secure, happy and more in control of my life. These ways of seeking happiness can be called the false self.

I believe that the concept of the false self is very important for the spiritual journey. The ground of all being is God. God is the source of my true self. The false self is the part of me that feels separated from God and thus seeks happiness in ways, which will never satisfy. The spiritual journey involves the death of the false self and the birth of the true self. The false self is fundamentally self-centred, seeking to bolster the fragile ego in every possible way. The false self flourishes in any environment and will seek to surround itself with the symbols of esteem, security and control that are prized in that environment. Therefore in a wealthy society, a person may seek to surround himself with cars or expensive clothes; in a poor environment, the individual might feel better about himself if he has a hen when his neighbours have none. Whatever the situation, the same process is at work.

The false self is at home in any situation. Under the domination of the false self we will seek happiness by collecting the symbols of esteem, security and control that are prized in our particular lifestyle. To outsiders these symbols may appear to be worthless but if our own group prizes them, then the false self can use them.

The false self will very happily wear a religious habit and live in a religious house so long as it can continue to live a self-centred life. The false self is the opponent to the work of God in us who desires to transform us. How can we recognise when the false self is at work in us? It is often not possible to see what is happening using reason because the false self has harnessed the gift of reason to support its own position. What gives it away are our emotions. Look at how you feel when you are challenged in some way or when things do not go according to your plans. The false self will kick in very quickly giving you plenty of reasons as to why you should feel angry or insulted and why you should not accept whatever is being said. We may think that we are very far down the road to sanctity but our emotions, especially when we are riled, will let us know what are our true values. So, humility, which is to know and accept the truth about ourselves, is a vital foundation for the spiritual journey but also must accompany us every step of the way.

The trouble with the false self is that these motivations are hidden from us unless we take seriously the call of Christ to follow him on the spiritual journey. Following Christ leads inevitably to the cross. In order that the true self, made in the image and likeness of God, may come to birth, the false self must die. This of course involves embracing the cross and passing through the dark night. A part of the darkness is caused when we begin to see that our motivation is not as holy as we thought it was and when we begin to understand how difficult it is to change it.

The false self can and will adapt itself to any way of life. The false self is that which seeks happiness in the wrong ways. The more "spiritual" we become, the subtler does the false self become. The false self seeks happiness through being in control of its own environment, through the acceptance of others and through one's own security. Perhaps at one time in our life we sought happiness in gross ways but now that God has become very important to us, we may think that we seek our happiness only in God. However, the false self does not lie down and die so easily. Basically it still seeks its happiness in the same ways only these ways are now modified to suit our more "spiritual" outlook.

Perhaps we may feel that John of the Cross' description of beginners has no relevance to us because we have left that stage behind a long time ago. Perhaps that is true or is it a sign of a lack of humility? The false self does not want us to know ourselves. Above all the false self does not want others to know us as we really are because then, it convinces us, they will reject us. In spiritual circles, the false self can adapt itself by presenting itself as being very spiritual. "I am quite advanced on the spiritual journey; I have many spiritual experiences, which I want to share with you. You should recognise me as a spiritual person and naturally I get upset when others do not recognise how advanced I am."

It is vital for us to begin to recognise when our false self is at work and to do something about it. This is true asceticism - much more difficult and much more fruitful than giving up sugar for Lent! We can become aware by leading a reflective life and listening to our emotions. Perhaps at the end of the day, we can look back at our experience and ask whether the cause of an emotional upset was righteous anger or because my pride was hurt. Gradually we can begin to notice the false self at work immediately. As soon as we become aware of the influence of the false self, we can offer to God our frustrated feelings and ask God to fill the gap with divine love.

The false self leads to misery and death and so transformation is essential. The spiritual journey is a journey of transformation in which the false self is put to death and the true self, made in the image and likeness of God, can come to birth. It is literally a matter of life and death for the one who seeks to save his life will lose it while the one who loses his life for the sake of the Gospel will save it.

The spiritual journey involves a continual struggle against the false self. It can be most subtle and can convince us that we have vanquished it once and for all. We are often not aware that the false self is operating at full throttle and indeed we think that we are doing very well.

I am convinced that what ties most good people down, what holds them back from journeying towards transformation is the belief that things are going just fine. "Yes, I am a sinner in need of God's mercy and yes, I have so much to learn from everyone and yes, I want nothing but God but don't whatever you do touch the image I have of myself." We can so easily play at spirituality; we can get up very early to pray, light our prayer candle piously and be there for an hour listening to the Lord and yet hear nothing because we have put spiritual cotton wool in our ears. God does not follow the paths that we lay out. "My ways are not your ways; my thoughts are not your thoughts". (Is.55, 8). I can quote that countless times and yet really not take it to heart. In practice it means that God will come to me in ways that I do not expect. The angel of God, which means God's messenger, will not have wings or be surrounded by a bright light. The angel of the Lord will come to me looking like the person whom I find difficult to accept. That person will bear God's word to me but can I accept this Word especially if it challenges what I hold dear, if it threatens my fragile self-image, my image of someone who is hardly a beginner in the spiritual life?

The Invitation

God invites us to enter on the great adventure of the spiritual journey and usually at the beginning the invitation comes in a very gentle way. However if God sees that I am serious about the journey, the gloves come off as it were. Then the testing time really begins. Am I prepared to face my dark side or will I use any means of escaping that confrontation? It would appear that some people are not at the stage where they can face themselves. In that case I believe that God gently invites the individual to that stage where the real healing begins. The most effective way of escaping the confrontation is to assume that I am doing fine or that I have already completed the task of conversion. This is the self that I want to face but not that one. I really want God's will to be done in me; I want to seek God's will but clearly God cannot be saying this or that.

The closer we allow God to come to us the clearer we see ourselves. We begin to be aware of the darker side of our personality and what used to be very clear in the past now becomes not so clear. God is not a thing to be manipulated and used for our gratification and therefore often seems to withdraw. At this time it can feel that we are going backwards and getting further away from God. Our weaknesses can become clearer and clearer both to ourselves and to others. Perhaps our general frustration with life will boil over from time to time and we will lash out against others. This will not at all seem to be the actions of one who is "spiritual". The image that we have of ourselves begins to crack and the image that we have so carefully cultivated and so carefully projected to others begins to appear rather threadbare. Usually of course we take out our frustrations on those who are close to us. So we might very well find ourselves having a real go at God who is refusing now to play the game according to our rules. God is not now acting the way we expect but so differently that we have great difficulty in believing that it is actually God who is at work at all.

If we are to proceed on the journey we must be prepared to risk all. Can we cut those fine, slender threads that are keeping us firmly anchored to the ground? They are very beautiful threads and we have an aversion to cutting them but if we do not cut them, we will never fly. The risk is to let go of my defences, to let them drop. It is a risky business. Look what happened when Pope John XXIII opened the windows a little to let some fresh air into the Church. For a time it was as if a hurricane had blown in. Things could never be the same again. Some people would like to close the window because it is safer that way and I suppose they are right; it is safer but we are not called to be safe. Remember what happened to the man who buried his one talent because he was afraid of the master. (Mt. 25, 14-30) God seems to like spiritual gamblers. To gamble is risky because you might lose everything. Some people prefer to be safe. "If anyone wants to be a follower of mine, let him renounce himself and take up his cross and follow me. For anyone who wants to save his life will lose it; but anyone who loses his life for my sake and the sake of the Gospel, will save it." (Mk. 8,34-35).

The false self, which surrounds us like a cocoon, must be destroyed so that we can experience the freedom of the children of God. The first step is therefore to recognise and accept what we truly are. If we do not, we will continue to live in a world of illusion. The false self is a master of disguise and seeks with all its power not to be dragged out into the light. We have so many ways of not hearing the call of the Gospel to repent and believe the Good News. The best way not to hear is to think that it does not apply to us because we are already converted. We can surround ourselves with all sorts of excuses for the way we live or for how we act in particular situations. We become so used to the little refusals to live the Gospel that we no longer notice the inconsistency. The false self will very easily persuade us that we are right and that some challenging part of the Gospel does not apply to us.

We have said that Lectio divina, or sacred reading of the Scriptures, is the most traditional way of growing in our relationship with God. God speaks to me through the Word and God's Word is creative; it gives life. However, the Word of God cuts more finely than a double-edged sword and it can lay bare what is false within us so that the true self can come to birth. (cf. Heb. 4,12).

It is very important to seek to be faithful to God in the circumstances of our own life, and God will lead us into the desert where we have to let go of all our supports in order to hear the voice of God who speaks to our hearts. In the desert, we come face to face with our false self; in the battle, there can be only one victor. The false self is a coward and does not want to have to fight and so will do all in its power to hide and not be brought into the light. The false self flourishes in the darkness because it belongs to the darkness but we are children of the light and in the light our true self can grow. We will become aware that all the old ways of seeking happiness were doomed to failure and that our hearts can only be satisfied in and by God.

Mount Carmel

The experience of the first hermits on Mount Carmel can be helpful as we seek to follow the same spiritual path as they did. The cell is an important concept in the Carmelite Rule and in later Carmelite writings. It represents the interior; it is where we come face to face with ourselves in order to fight the enemy. For this battle we need the protection of the armour of God.[59] The Rule of St. Albert has a dynamic of moving from the individual cell to the chapel at the centre of all the cells and then returning to the solitude of the cell. Listening to the Word of God and celebrating Eucharist together strengthen all of us to return to the struggle in the cell and from our struggles with the false self in the silence of the cell, we bring a purified heart to the service of the others.

A certain amount of interior silence is an essential weapon in the struggle with the false self and therefore in the process of purification because, away from many distractions, we come face to face with ourselves as we really are. We begin to see through the elaborate façade that we have spent many years building up to protect our fragile egos. We begin to become aware of the infidelities, big and small in our lives and the great inconsistency between the ideals that we profess and the reality we live. Clearly the cell is a spiritual concept and not necessarily a concrete place; it is the place of encounter with God in the depths of our being. Each individual, no matter what his or her state in life, is called to encounter God who dwells within.

Reading the Gospels is important to find out what Jesus actually says but it is only when we come to silence that we give God the opportunity to pierce beyond our own words and thoughts and speak directly to our hearts.

When we are silent, we have the chance to be retuned onto God's wavelength. Very often during the time of prayer nothing seems to happen but if we are tuned into God, we will pick up all sorts of things outside the time of prayer. Much of what we will pick up will not be to our liking or will go against our preconceived notions. At times we can be covered in complete confusion and God can seem to disappear. God desires to transform us from within so that we become like God; we become a channel of God's revelation to the world. This is what God desires to do but this is a long process and hard because if this is to take place the false self must die so that the true self which is created in the image of God can come to birth.

All of this is so confusing because we have an idea of what holiness is and none of our experiences seem to fit in with our ideas at all. God takes the carpet from under us. There will be a real temptation to return to a way of prayer where we felt good and where we felt that we were making progress. God is so far beyond our human concepts that we cannot grasp hold of God and what God desires to do within us is so beyond us that we cannot grasp that either. Yet

---

[59] Rule, 18 & 19

while all this confusion is surrounding us, there will be at our deepest level a vague feeling that somehow or other something good is happening and indeed it is. It is the greatest blessing of our lives although it seems to be anything but a blessing.

We will be able to hear God's voice in the most unusual circumstances e.g. someone will say something to us or about us which may annoy us but we will be able to accept the truth of it much more easily than before. God will become more and more important to us even though it seems that God has disappeared entirely. We begin to anxiously search for God.

All these surprises and all this confusion lead to a slow dying of the false self. Perhaps it will only be after our physical death that the true self will be seen in all its glory. During our time here on earth, let us trust in God who is at work within us. If we go along with God's action within us, we will become less and less surprised at God's ways.

One Dark Night

God pursues us, courts us, gives us "wake up" calls in order that we continue our journey towards our centre who is God. This process, taken as a whole, can be called the dark night and is a vital element in the process of transformation. It is a classic concept in spiritual theology and a classic Carmelite concept.

In the dark night, the false self is broken down gradually. The dark night is an effect of the impact of God's love on our lives. We cannot say how the dark night will develop but normally the first part is generally when we ourselves set out on the spiritual journey with enthusiasm and dedication. We begin gradually to reorganise our lives around the message of Jesus Christ. We give up obviously sinful areas in our lives. This can be painful but often the pain is submerged in the initial joy of following Christ. Once we begin to get used to being Christian or being Carmelite, there is the danger of settling down but God will not allow that to happen, at least not without a struggle. God always works with human nature.

If we are serious about doing God's will and trying our best to put it into practice in daily life, we will soon come across major obstacles within ourselves to the fulfilment of God's will. Our false self will rebel against any attempt to attack it head on. This internal battle causes darkness. This darkness can be painful, but if we try to remain faithful, it is a healing darkness because God is present in the darkness healing the wounds, which the false self has inflicted, and setting us free to be what God created us to be.

What are these obstacles within us, which cause so much trouble? The false self-system is based on a lie and the lie is that if we receive enough esteem and affection, if we have enough security in our lives, and if we can control our lives, we will be happy. Since we are created with an infinite capacity, we then seek infinite amounts of affection, security and control. When our interest turns from worldly things to religious things, the false self simply moves its focus also.

The dark night brings us to a greater awareness of who we are and how attached we are to our own ideas for happiness. It is a very important part of the transformation process because this experience helps us to let go of those ideas for happiness, which actually lead to misery. A major reason for the darkness is that we let go of our own ideas of how to attain happiness and we are still not receiving the fullness of happiness from God. This is an invitation to wait in the darkness for God who is faithful. The darkness gets deeper as the love of God reaches the most interior parts of the soul but the darker the night, the nearer is the dawn. The dark night is not a punishment but a sign of God's love and a guarantee that God is at work within us setting us free to be ourselves. The dark night is an essential stage on our journey towards freedom. It is important to co-operate with God's work. At times the only co-operation possible is faith and silent love.

The process of transformation is a long one because it is a radical change of the human being. Transformation is not just a change in the person to allow him or her to live a good, Christian life. It is a radical change so that we might become what we were created to be – like God.

There is a deep hunger in the human heart. Nothing is ever enough; we are always seeking more. It is the Christian understanding of life that we are made for God and only God can satisfy the infinite hunger of the human heart. The tragedy of human existence is that so often we seek to assuage this raging hunger and thirst with what is not God. These things may satisfy us for a time but not forever.[60]

To be transformed means to attain our destiny insofar as this is possible here on earth and to become what we were created to be.

---

[60] See J. Welch, *The Seasons of the Heart*, talk given to the General Chapter of the Order of Carmelites, September 2001, published in CITOC, No. 5, September-October 2001, p. 119. It is also available at http://www.carmelite.org/welch/soh1.htm

We were created to walk with God in paradise. Through the redemption won for us by Jesus Christ, we are God's beloved children. Christ is the prototype of a new humanity; we are to become like him and so incarnate some aspect of the divine in human flesh. This is God's work. No amount of effort on our part will bring this about unless God accomplishes it but equally God will not bring about our transformation without our co-operation. The work of transformation is a mysterious co-operation between the human being and the divine working together to produce God's work of art, which is the transformed man or woman.

CHAPTER FOUR

TOWARDS CONTEMPLATION

The word "contemplatio" is the Latin rendering of the Greek "theoria", an attempt to translate the Hebrew "da'ath", which refers to a loving knowledge of God. The word "contemplation" in the strict sense does not appear in the Scriptures but if we understand contemplation as the search for union with God, then clearly the whole Bible is focused on this – the human and divine relationship. Pope Gregory the Great summed up the teaching of the preceding six Christian centuries by emphasising the role of love and knowledge in the work of contemplation. According to Gregory the Great: "...The fundamental preparation for contemplation, of course, is the devout living of the Christian life through the power of the Holy Spirit expressed in the virtues of faith, hope and charity and the increasing activity of the sevenfold gift."[61] The supreme value of Christianity is not contemplation but love. For Teresa of Avila, the spiritual journey is not confined to our experiences in prayer. "It is necessary that your foundation consist of more than prayer and contemplation. If you do not strive for the virtues and practice them, you will always be dwarfs."[62]

When we speak of contemplation, there is a danger that we can become utterly confused because of the connections that it may have in our minds. Contemplative prayer is for everybody. It should be the normal flowering of a friendship with Christ, which begins with our baptism. It has nothing to do with visions or levitations or heavenly words spoken to us. Being put off contemplative prayer because of things like that is like refusing to eat lettuce because some people are allergic to it. I am sure that some people are but the vast majority of people are not.

In recent years there has been an increasing interest in prayer. Prayer groups have sprung up all over the place and people have

---

[61] McGinn, Bernard, *The Growth of Mysticism, The Presence of God: A History of Western Christian Mysticism Series* (SCM Press, London, 1994) Vol. II, p.56

[62] *Interior Castle*, 7,4,9. She wrote earlier in the same treatise, "When I see souls very earnest in trying to understand the prayer they have and very sullen when they are in it – for it seems they don't dare let their minds move or stir lest a bit of their spiritual delight and devotion be lost – it makes me realise how little they understand of the way by which union is attained; they think the whole matter lies in these things. No, Sisters, absolutely not; works are what the Lord wants!" (Interior Castle, 5,3,11).

been introduced to various forms of prayer. In our Christian tradition, there is an immensely rich tradition of prayer. We need to try to get back to the traditional Christian path where contemplative prayer was not reserved for an elite few.

There are many definitions of contemplative prayer. Mine is simply intimate friendship with God. Each one of us by our baptism has been called to be the intimate friends of God. This is not something reserved for the great saints. It is for everyone. The daffodil bulb that is planted in the ground is intended to become a daffodil. If it does not, there is something wrong. It is perfectly natural for the bulb to grow into a beautiful daffodil. Just so, it is perfectly natural for us to grow in our relationship with God until we become intimate friends.

Contemplation is not an end in itself; it is a means to arrive at union with God. Contemplation is not the reward for great virtue or much time spent in prayer but is that which makes us capable of great virtue, of great love. However, the readiness to encounter God immediately and directly in contemplation normally presupposes perseverance at some discursive prayer for a considerable length of time.

Contemplation and the Carmelite Rule

The words "contemplation" or "contemplative prayer" do not appear in the Carmelite Rule. Instead other terms appear like, "meditating day and night on the Word of the Lord" (10); "your breast is to be fortified by holy ponderings" (19); "The sword of the spirit, which is the word of God, should dwell abundantly in your mouth and in your hearts" (19); "The apostle recommends silence, when he tells us to work in it. As the prophet also testifies, silence is the cultivation of justice and again, in silence and hope will be your strength" (21); "let him try attentively and carefully to practice the silence in which is the cultivation of justice." (21).[63]

At the time of the writing of the Rule, there was not much concern about defining stages of prayer. When the 12th century Carthusian, Guigo II wrote about the four steps of reading, meditation, prayer and contemplation, they were intended as teaching aids for young people who joined monastic communities; they were never

---

[63] The translation of the Carmelite Rule is that of K. Waaijman, *The Mystical Space of Carmel*, (Peeters, Leuven, 1999), p.29-38

intended to be hard and fast definitions.[64] Lectio Divina was the normal way of prayer for monastics and it was intended to lead to transformation in Christ. Meditation at this time had nothing to do with discursive thinking about God and the things of God; instead it was a practice whereby the whole body became involved in the prayer. The hermits would murmur the words of the psalms and repeat them over and over until such times as the words took root within them and they would come spontaneously to mind during their daily work. Clearly St. Albert had meditated long on the Word of God because the Rule is full of Scriptural allusions and direct quotes. The Word of God is part of him and so becomes the heart of the Rule which he wrote.

Our way of praying is different from that of those first hermits because our life is different but the goal is the same. The concept of contemplation has been deeply affected by the history of spirituality. As a result of various historical factors, contemplation came to be looked upon with grave suspicion. We know the difficulties, which both St. John of the Cross and St. Teresa had with the Inquisition because of the general suspicion that surrounded contemplation. This suspicion lasted for about 400 years and some of the effects are still with us. One of the most grave effects was that contemplation was cut off from the vast majority of the Christian people and was reserved for an elite group. There was no teaching or preaching about the goal of Christian prayer and most people had never heard of contemplation. This has been partly remedied in recent years with the upsurge of interest in prayer. Many Christians turned towards the Eastern religions because they could find no spiritual depth within Christianity. It has been said that if you visit any Buddhist community in the West, you will find that half of the members are former Catholics. Thank God, this situation evoked a response among Christians and now there are a number of movements that teach the Christian contemplative tradition.

The Rule does not teach contemplative prayer; no one can teach contemplative prayer. Lectio Divina was never just a way of prayer; it was and is a way of life. The four phases of Lectio Divina – reading, meditation, prayer and contemplation – flow in and out of each other and form a seamless whole.   The hermits did not have four separate times during which they read the Scriptures, meditated on them, prayed about them and then contemplated. They read the

---

[64] *The Ladder of the Monks and the Twelve Meditations*, op. cit.

Word of God while alone in their cells and while together for meals and for the celebration of the Eucharist or for the recitation of the psalms. Those who could not read, recited the Our Father and Hail Mary, both of course Scriptural prayers. They meditated the Word of God, murmuring the words over and over in their cells or at work outside and so the Word became part of them. This led spontaneously to prayer arising from the heart as a response to the Word that they heard. The response could be thanksgiving, repentance, praise or whatever. Contemplative moments could emerge at any point during the day when God took over and the hermits let go of their own words, their own thoughts, their own emotions.

We cannot live or pray the way the hermits on Mt. Carmel did. The simple reason is that 800 years of history separate us. They were medieval people and we are not. We cannot pray as if the world were flat or as if our world had not become a global village. The hermits had no idea that large parts of our world even existed. We must be concerned about what is happening in other parts of our world because human beings, our brothers and sisters, are affected. The hermits were children of their age and we are children of our age. When we study the Rule, we are not trying to copy the life of the hermits; we are seeking the values that inspired them and allowing these same values to inspire us also.

Having said that, the goal of our prayer is the same as that of the first hermits on Mount Carmel. We seek to pray unceasingly, to live in the presence of God, to be so in tune with God that everything we do or say or think is according to the will of God. The Rule puts it this way, "The sword of the spirit, the word of God, should dwell abundantly in your mouth and in your hearts. And whatever you do, let it all be done in the Word of the Lord."[65]

When we consider contemplation and contemplative prayer, we of course must take into account what the great mystics have said about it, for example St. John of the Cross said that we seek in reading and we find in meditation; we knock in prayer and it is opened to us in contemplation.[66] The first three elements are active – what we can do – and the last, contemplation is passive – what God does. Contemplation is not confined to a specific time of prayer. According to John, contemplation begins with the dark night of sense, which is not at all an elevated state. Contemplation then begins

---

[65] *Rule* 19
[66] *Maxims on Love*, 79

when we take the spiritual journey seriously and with our whole heart try to respond to God's invitation to intimacy. God then draws us further and begins to take over the process of transforming us in Christ. At the beginning stages we are still very active, avoiding sin, doing good works, saying our prayers and so on but as the relationship with God develops into a firm friendship, our efforts become less important than our trust in God. We have very many lessons to learn on this journey and many ways of acting to unlearn. There are many potholes on this road and also many interesting deviations from the straight and narrow path.

As we are growing in intimacy with God, our prayer is beginning to change. There is a subtle and gradual movement from our effort to God's work. Of course God is at work in any authentic prayer but as we grow in intimacy with God, so God gradually begins to take over the steering wheel. The driver determines where the car goes. If we try to interfere with the driving, we will crash. Obviously it is important to determine who is going to drive the car. If we simply let go of the steering wheel and God does not take over, we will also crash. At this point, the famous three signs of John of the Cross come into play. These are signs pointing to when a person ought to give up discursive meditation and pass on to the state of contemplation. The first sign is the realisation that one cannot make discursive meditation nor receive satisfaction from it as before. Dryness is the result of trying to meditate on subjects that formerly gave satisfaction. The second sign is an awareness of a disinclination to fix the imagination upon particular objects, either exterior or interior. The third and surest sign is that a person wants to remain alone in loving awareness of God, without particular considerations, in interior peace and quiet.[67] In the book of the Dark Night, the three signs are given from another perspective, that of judging whether the dryness that a person is experiencing comes from God's action.[68]

Those three signs are written with a particular understanding of meditation as discursive reflection. I doubt whether many people actually meditate in that sense any more. However, I think that the term meditation in John's understanding includes any kind of prayer where we are active. After that comes contemplation, which is the work of God, not ours. God determines when and if it happens, not us.

---

[67] *Ascent of Mt. Carmel*, II, 13, 2-4
[68] *Dark Night*, I, 9

The Carmelite Rule does not teach contemplative prayer; it prepares the way for it. The Rule provides the elements of a spiritually healthy way of life that leads people towards transformation in Christ. The Rule, as we have said, assumes the rhythm of Lectio Divina, which leads towards contemplation. We can decide to read the Word of God and to ponder on it. Our response to the Word is usually spontaneous and the fruit of what has gone before but nevertheless we are still in control. Contemplative prayer happens to us. We have no control when it comes to contemplative prayer. This is God's action and we are put to sleep in a sense while God, the great Physician, operates deep within us to transform those hidden recesses of our hearts into the image of Christ. The process of contemplation goes on in daily life but reaches a high point in contemplative prayer. At the beginning contemplation is so vague and so gentle that the individual will normally be unaware that anything unusual is taking place. In some people this awareness grows enormously and we can see the results of this contemplative awareness in the abundance of mystical literature throughout the centuries.

The medieval mind was rather different to ours. We have a mania for thinking things out, planning for the future, dwelling on the past. Our minds do not stop; we have an internal tape or CD that accompanies us throughout the day with incessant noise. We are either commenting on this or reacting to that. Often our prayer is simply part of this incessant noise and is not truly an opening of our whole being to the Living God. We want to follow our own agenda instead of responding to the gentle invitation of God to enter into the intimate life of the Blessed Trinity. The central point of Christianity is that we are called into an intimate relationship with God in and through Jesus Christ. In this relationship we are transformed and become what God knows we can be, like God, able to see creation with the eyes of God and love creation with God's heart.

Intimacy with God

Contemplation is a process of growing in relationship with God. We have been called to intimacy with God. The process of contemplation takes place within the whole of life; every aspect of life is involved as we grow in intimacy with God. Humility and honesty are essential on this journey. We need to have a profound desire that God's will be accomplished in and through us, otherwise we will give up when the going gets a little rough. The process of growing in intimacy with God is at the same time a process of purification. Our human ways of thinking, loving and acting are gradually, piece by piece, transformed into divine ways. The light of God's Word shines a powerful light into the dark corners of our heart. It is very difficult to accept what becomes clear in the light but if we do, we can be set free to become what God knows we can be. We are called to be contemplatives, which I believe simply means to be mature friends of Jesus Christ. We cannot pretend to answer God's call to enter into intimacy unless we make a commitment to prayer, which does not mean talking at God but above all listening to God.

The Pope, in his Apostolic Letter "Novo Millennio Ineunte", to mark the closing of the jubilee year 2000 and the opening of the new millennium[60] stresses that holiness, which is "a message that convinces without the need for words"[70] calls for "a Christian life distinguished above all in the art of prayer".[71] He speaks of a widespread demand for spirituality as one of the "signs of the times"[72] and that our Christian communities must become genuine schools of prayer which teach people to express their relationship with Christ in various ways "until the heart truly falls in love".[73]

The Pope also says that people today, though perhaps unconsciously, express the same request that certain Greeks made to Philip, "We want to see Jesus" (Jn.12,21). We are asked not only to speak of Christ but in a certain sense to "show" him to them.[74]

Lectio Divina, which has been regaining much of its popularity in recent years, was intended to lead to this loving knowledge of God. With the rise of scholasticism and the tendency to divide and examine each element in isolation from the others, the natural flow of Lectio Divina towards contemplation became stuck in the area of discursive meditation. All sorts of methods of meditation were laboriously worked out and contemplation tended to be reserved for an elite group within the Church. It was generally thought to be out of the reach of ordinary people and indeed dangerous for them. This tendency was reinforced by various movements that arose rejecting the sacramental, hierarchical, institutional Church for a nebulous

---

[69] 6th January, 2001
[70] Para. 30
[71] Para. 32
[72] Para. 33
[73] *Ibid*
[74] Para. 16

individual illumination from on high, which exempted individuals even from basic Christian morality.

Teresa of Avila and John of the Cross lived at a time of great ferment in the Church and in Spanish society. The Counter Reformation, spearheaded by the recently founded Company of Jesus, was in full swing, and with the "discovery" of America, there was a great desire to win souls for Christ. Women's choices were severely restricted and the only way they could take part in this evangelisation was either to produce sons who would go there or they could pray. However, even in the area of prayer they were restricted. The Inquisition was very suspicious of women who strayed outside the narrow confines of vocal prayer. Because of the suspicion that was cast on contemplation and which remained in the Church for several centuries, most people were actively discouraged from any kind of silent prayer. St. Teresa showed how one could become a great contemplative by reciting the Our Father.[75] God cannot be defeated by human regulations. There was a general dissatisfaction with the strict meditations of the past where one had to pass from point to point. That was certainly not what St. Albert had in mind when he wrote the Rule nor what the hermits had in mind when they made their proposal to him.

However "mental prayer" was very much in vogue and Teresa learned a method of prayer which helped her enormously. She began to have experiences in prayer and had the gift of being able to describe these clearly. St. John of the Cross, on the other hand, expressed his experience of God in poetry and his prose works are a theological explanation of what is contained in the poems.

Teresa and John received their formation in the Carmelite Order whose goal was defined in the Institution of the First Monks (a very well known text at the time):

"The goal of this life is twofold: One part we acquire by our own effort and the exercise of the virtues, with the help of divine grace. This is to offer God a heart that is holy and pure from actual stain of sin. We attain this goal when we are perfect and 'in Carith', that is, hidden in that charity of which the Wise Man says: 'Love covers all offences' (Pr. 10,12). Wishing Elijah to reach this goal, God said to him, 'Hide in the wadi Carith'. The other goal of this life is granted to us as the free gift of God; namely, not only after death but even in this mortal life, to taste somewhat in the heart and to experience

---

[75] *Way of Perfection*, 25

in the mind the power of the divine presence and the sweetness of heavenly glory."[76] It seems that this may have been written in the late 14th century but in the time of Teresa and John, it was thought to predate the Rule of St. Albert. John was obviously well read in the area of mysticism and seems to have been deeply affected by the apophatic teaching of Pseudo-Dyonysius. Whatever the effects of their formation, it is certain that both Teresa and John are original spiritual giants whose writings have dominated the history of spirituality ever since.

Even before Teresa and John, contemplation was understood in terms of prayer. Teresa wrote about the stages of contemplative prayer beginning with the prayer of quiet and ending with the experience of spiritual marriage. John's description of the experience of the dark night seems to express a universal element of the spiritual path. However, it would be a grave mistake to think that the spiritual journey is the same for everyone. God cannot be confined to human concepts and often acts completely outside our notions. The spiritual journey is unique to each individual since it is an individual relationship with God. However, the elements of the journey provided by John of the Cross are signposts that one is on the right path.

The Catechism of the Catholic Church understands prayer as primarily a relationship with God and only secondly as a specific activity.[77] Based on the long Christian contemplative tradition, the Catechism describes contemplation in the following ways:

> "Contemplative prayer is the prayer of the child of God, of the forgiven sinner who agrees to welcome the love by which he is loved and who wants to respond to it by loving even more (Cf. Lk 7:36-50,19:1-10). But he knows that the love he is returning is poured out by the Spirit in his heart, for everything is grace from God. Contemplative prayer is the poor and humble surrender to the loving will of the Father in ever deeper union with his beloved Son.
>
> Contemplative prayer is the simplest expression of the mystery of prayer. It is a gift, a grace; it can be accepted only in humility and poverty. Contemplative prayer is a covenant relationship established by God within our hearts (Cf. Jer 31:33). Contemplative prayer is a communion in which the Holy Trinity conform man, the image of God, 'to his likeness'.
>
> Contemplative prayer is *silence*, the 'symbol of the world to come'

---

[76] Book 1, chap. 2

[77] *Catechism of the Catholic Church*, (Geoffrey Chapman, London, 1994), Art. 2558

or 'silent love'. Words in this kind of prayer are not speeches; they are like kindling that feeds the fire of love. In this silence, unbearable to the 'outer' man, the Father speaks to us his incarnate Word, who suffered, died and rose; in this silence the Spirit of adoption enables us to share in the prayer of Jesus."[78]

Contemplation is the irruption of God in the human soul. It is a silent, imageless and loving communion with God, which transcends all discursiveness. "Contemplation is none other than a secret, peaceful and loving infusion of God which, if the soul allows it to happen, enflames it in the spirit of love."[79] "Secret contemplation .. is a science of love...which is an infused loving knowledge, that both illumines and enamours the soul, elevating it step by step unto God its Creator."[80]

It is clear that contemplation is infused, i.e. it comes from God and cannot be grasped by us. "So delicate is this interior refreshment that ordinarily if one desires it or tries to experience it, it will not be experienced because, as I say, it does its work when the soul is most at rest and most free from care; it is like the air which, if one desires to close one's hand upon it, escapes."[81] Commentators on Teresa and John raised the issue of whether contemplation could be acquired. This started a great debate among spiritual theologians. It is agreed that the state reached by human effort could not be compared to infused contemplation, which is qualitatively different from any way of prayer which has preceded it. Contemplation is a kind of conversation with no intermediary and no possibility of misunderstanding the communication. In contemplation, God does not come through the senses or through the normal pattern of knowing. God comes from an unknown way infusing directly into our being a loving knowledge of Him.

In contemplation our normal ways of knowing and understanding are stilled and at first there can be the feeling of anxiety that we are doing nothing. So contemplation is a strange new land where everything natural to us seems to be turned upside down, where we learn a new language, the language of silence. We learn a new way of being, not to be always doing but simply to be, where our thoughts and concepts, our imagination, senses and feelings are abandoned for faith in what is unseen and unfelt, where God's seem-

---

[78] *Ibid*, Arts. 2712, 2713, 2717
[79] John of the Cross, *Dark Night*, 1,10,6
[80] *Ibid.*, 2, 18,5
[81] *Ibid.*, 1,9,6

ing absence to our senses is God's presence and God's silence to our ordinary perception is God's speech. It is entering into the unknown, letting go of everything familiar we would cling to for security. Entering this new land at first is like entering darkness and emptiness. It is entering into a process, which is a kind of death but this is the death that Jesus tells us leads to life.[82]

Contemplation begins when we entrust ourselves to God, in whatever way God chooses to approach us; it is an attitude of openness to God, whose presence we discover in all things. Thus, contemplation is an inner journey, arising out of the free initiative of God, who touches and transforms us, leading us towards unity of love with him, raising us up so that we may enjoy this gratuitous love and live in his loving presence. It is a transforming experience of the overpowering love of God. This love empties us of our limited and imperfect human ways of thinking, loving, and behaving, transforming them into divine ways.[83]

Prayer is the door to contemplation and without prayer we cannot hope to lead any kind of spiritual life. I am convinced, however, that contemplation is much more than prayer but the heart of the matter is prayer. It is a process of transformation, which leads the human being to become a new creation by being transformed in God. The process of transformation is a gradual growth of the human being in the image and likeness of God and this process is a constant factor in the mystical tradition. [84] Transformation cannot occur without the old, false self dying so that the new self, formed in the image of Christ, can grow. The darkness of the death of the false self becomes the dawn and new day of the new creation. Towards the end of the document on the Consecrated Life, the Pope exhorts consecrated people, "Do not forget that you, in a very special way, can and must say that you not only belong to Christ but that 'you have become Christ'."[85]

---

[82] Cf. Mt. 10,39; Mk. 8,35; Lk. 9,24; Jn.12,25

[83] Constitutions of the Brothers of the Blessed Virgin Mary of Mount Carmel, (Carmelite General Curia, 25th March, 1996), no.17

[84] H. Blommestijn & K. Waaijman O.Carm, L'Homme Spirituel a L'Image de Dieu Selon Jean de la Croix, in Juan de la Cruz, Espiritu de Llama, Vacare Deo X, Studies in Spirituality Supp. 1, Institutum Carmelitanum, Rome & Kok Pharos Publishing House, Netherlands, p. 623-656. See also in regard to the teaching of St. John of the Cross, H. Blommestijn, K. Waaijman & J. Huls, In the Footsteps of Love, (Peeters, Leuven, 2001).

[85] Vita Consecrata, 109 quoting St. Augustine, Treatise on St. John's Gospel, XXI, 8: Pl 35, 1568. This document was published on 25th March 1996 after the Synod of Bishops on the same topic.

The journey through the desert, a very important theme in Carmelite tradition, is contemplation. God uses every element of life in the great work of transformation. St. Thérèse of Lisieux intuitively understood this fundamental fact and so welcomed all the events of life as coming from the hand of God.

It is most important to be aware that the events of daily life are part and parcel of the spiritual journey. How often do we react to these events taking no account of God? If I find some situation a little difficult, it is too easy to go my own way instead of seeking God's will in whatever difficult situation I may find myself. Trying to do God's will in daily life is not easy since it involves a constant battle against selfishness which is part of all of us. It means looking on the little contradictions we meet every day with the eyes of faith. This daily asceticism is an essential part of the Christian life and no growth can be expected in prayer if we are not willing to grow up in dealing with the ordinary events of life.

Death and Resurrection

The call to contemplation is not for the faint-hearted; it is not for those who seek spiritual experiences. Contemplation leads to death, the death of all that is false within us which is in fact liberation, but which must be experienced as death first of all. Thomas Merton also had a passionate desire for truth. He described contemplation in the following terms:

> "If we set out into this darkness, we have to meet these inexorable forces. We will have to face fears and doubts. We will have to call into question the whole structure of our spiritual life. We will have to make a new evaluation of our motives for belief, for love, for self-commitment to the invisible God. At this moment, precisely, all spiritual light is darkened, all values lose their shape and reality, and we remain so to speak, suspended in the void."[86]

As God reveals to us the hidden motivation of our hearts, we discover that our faith, hope and love are in need of radical purification. Our reasons for believing, hoping and loving seem no longer to be valid or at least no longer sufficient. At the beginning of a good spiritual life, we will have given ourselves to God, as we have perceived God to be. We will have built up a structure for our spiritual lives, a structure with which we feel comfortable, which sup-

---

[86] *Contemplative Prayer*, (Image Books, Doubleday, New York, 1990) p.77

ports our image of who God is and what it means to lead a spiritual life. At a certain point this structure will begin to shake because it is in fact built on sand. It seems that if we seriously desire to stand in the truth, our faith, hope and love must be utterly purified. It seems that God disappears and leaves us in a more profound darkness than we have ever experienced before. At this time we cannot turn away from God even though it may feel that God has turned away from us. We cannot go backwards and yet we cannot seem to go forwards. We seem to be suspended in a void.

The reason for this experience, I would hazard to suggest, is that there is no point in replacing one set of human reasons for faith, hope and love with another set no matter how deep these latter reasons may be. The only valid foundation for surrendering oneself into the hands of the Invisible God is simply that God is. Therefore, it is in the darkness that I learn who God is. In God's time the darkness will reveal itself as God's presence.

The contemplative life is not a series of sublime spiritual experiences but involves the stripping of all that is false so that one stands naked before the Living God. At times this involves dread and anguished doubt but there is nothing in heaven or on earth which can compare to the gift of God which is given to the one who truly consents to God's presence and action. The contemplative life is a process of dying and rising. Without the death of the false self, there can be no resurrection. The resurrection is pure gift; there is nothing the human being can do to merit it. We can only wait in darkness trusting that it is God's good pleasure to give us the Kingdom (Lk. 12,32).

Every human being is called to holiness.[87] St. Thérèse of Lisieux understood that to be a saint meant to be totally available to the radical demands of love whatever that might entail. However when God who is love begins to make demands on us, we begin to realise our own poverty. All the grand illusions of an earlier period of the spiritual journey begin to crumble. Thérèse realised that she could not accomplish her desires. The mountain was just too high and the paths too steep. She desired to love God more than God had ever been loved before. She seized the smallest opportunity to show her love but despite all this she realised that she could not attain her desire. Through her experience of several years of failure to live up to her ideals she gained a new and vital insight into the spiritual journey. She never lowered her ideals to make them more easily

---

[87] *Lumen Gentium*, 5, 40

attainable. Instead she learned that it was God's good pleasure to lift her to the top of the mountain. In order for this to happen she could place no trust in herself but all her trust had to be placed in God. She learned that she could not pile up merits in the sight of God. She would appear before God with empty hands and she had complete confidence that God would fill her hands to overflowing. She would do everything in her power to please Jesus and he would look after the rest.

Our faith and hope must be placed in God but God is beyond all human conception. The ideas we have of God, no matter how noble they may seem to be, are not God because God is beyond any idea we could have. God's self-revelation comes to us through creation but even from all the wonders of the world we receive a very limited picture of God. The self-revelation of God continues through the experience of the Chosen People and the final and complete revelation of God comes to us through Jesus Christ. However in Christ there are inexhaustible treasures and we will never plumb the depths of Christ. God teaches us in the darkness. In the darkness our faith, hope and love are purified so that we will cling only to God and not to any human ideas no matter how inspiring these may have appeared at one time in our lives.[88]

Contemplation for all

The contemplative path for a very small minority of people involves all sorts of strange phenomena but for the vast majority of people, the process of transformation takes place under cover of darkness in prayer and in daily life. Whether one experiences something that enters into a classical definition of contemplation or mystical experience, I do not believe is important. What is vital is that we consent to what God desires to do in us. This consent is given in our prayer and in daily life.

Contemplation is a process of transformation. We may never know whether we are contemplatives or not but it will become clear to other people whether we are growing in the Christian life by the way we treat them for we shall look upon creation with the eyes of God and love all that has been created with God's own heart.

---

[88] For Thérèse's teaching on the purification of faith and hope, see *Ms.C*,5v and for the purification of love, see *Ms.C*,11v. These are to be found in the third part of *The Story of a Soul*.

If contemplation is really for everyone and is not reserved for those with a great deal of leisure time, it must be possible in the midst of a busy life. It is of course all very well talking about the glories of contemplation or the need for it but what can we do about it practically in the midst of our busy lives? The first and most important thing to remember is that contemplation is God's work and God's gift which is freely given whenever and to whomever God wishes. Responding to the grace of God, we entrust ourselves into the arms of God who loves us - we may not necessarily feel this but we believe it. We can prepare the way for the Lord like John the Baptist by examining our lives and seeing if there is anything that is incompatible with our vocation. We can then use the normal remedies that we are offered through the Church. However perhaps we are not ready to change or perhaps there are some elements of our character, which we cannot change at present. That need not hold us back. God is far greater than our weaknesses and God's mercy is more powerful than our sins and defects.

CHAPTER FIVE

SILENT PRAYER

The spiritual journey involves more than just the time we give to prayer; it involves the whole of life. It involves us in a process of purification and transformation so that we become one with Christ. God takes us as we are. Looking back at our lives, we have come to this point through various ups and downs. We have all been hurt, betrayed, let down; we have all been disappointed. We all have a choice as to how we are going to respond to our experience of life. Will we respond in faith or as those who live in a practical atheism, that is without any reference to God? Responding in faith means accepting our experience of life, the bad times as well as the good, and renewing our consent to God's presence and action in our lives. God does not necessarily cause the suffering that we have had to endure throughout our lives but God writes straight with crooked lines. God uses the circumstances of our life to purify us and continue the sacred work of transformation in us. "We know that God makes all things work together for the good of those who love him who have been called according to his decree." (Rom. 8,28)

God is at work within each of us but asks for our co-operation. Prayer is the time when we consciously co-operate with God's plan for us and it is prayer, which gives us the possibility of co-operating in the midst of our many activities. There are different types of prayer- liturgical, community, personal. There is an external aspect to prayer, especially to liturgical and community prayer but that is not the only aspect nor even the most important. In liturgical prayer, we join with the whole Church to give praise to God and to pray for the whole world. One aspect of liturgical prayer is to bring about a change in the participants. The externals are important but what is going on within our hearts is vital. If our community and liturgical prayer does not have some effect on each of us as individuals and on our relationships with others, there is something wrong. Perhaps we are following the correct rules and regulations but if there is no personal involvement in what is happening in the liturgy and no desire to change, we are not allowing the liturgy to do its work.

We also need an adequate time of personal prayer in our lives. This time is for an intimate conversation with the One whom we know loves us. If we think that we can get along quite well without personal prayer, we are very much mistaken. If we use the excuse of our important work to avoid the intimate dialogue with God, we are running away. Perhaps we need to ask ourselves what are we running away from?   St. Teresa of Avila was aware that giving up prayer was the biggest temptation of her life.[89]

It is only when we begin to let go of external distractions that we can become aware of the constant noise going on within us. When we begin to approach nearer to the innermost room of the castle, it is as if the enemy becomes even more frantic to keep us away. We have all sorts of distractions in our head. When we try to pray, we usually shut off as many external distractions as we can but then we become aware of all the internal noise. Sometimes our prayer can seem to be a constant battle against distractions. At other times, we may not even recognise that we are following a distraction instead of remaining with God. We may think that a point we are meditating on is very holy but it may in fact be a subtle way of reinforcing our own ego.

St. Teresa said that mental prayer, as she called it, began when we started to think of the person we were addressing when we prayed. Indeed she said that if we did not think of God when we prayed, it was difficult to call what we were doing prayer.[90] So some sort of reflection is an essential part of prayer. In that way we begin to apply the Gospel to our own situation and the foundations for a friendship with the Lord are laid. At some point there is a breakthrough and God touches our hearts. Then we respond from the heart to God. Now we can say that we have the beginnings of a friendship with God. All that has gone before has been an essential preparation for this stage. Without the preparation we are building our house on sand.

Our whole lives, and especially our prayer, must be a preparation for this transforming encounter with God. It is important to cultivate silence, both interior and exterior, even in the midst of the busiest life, so that we can truly hear the Word of God in the depths of our being. The voice of the Spirit is very gentle and we need to be very silent in order to hear it. According to St. John of the Cross, the language that God best hears is silent love.[91] Teresa said that the point of prayer is not to think much but to love much.[92] Silence is actually difficult to arrive at but is worth the effort because only in

---

[89] See *Life*, 7 & 8
[90] *Way of Perfection* 21,1
[91] *Maxims and Counsels*, 53
[92] *Foundations* 5,2 and *Interior Castle* 4,1,7

silence can we hear the Word, which is spoken by God in an eternal silence.

There comes a time when we need to lay aside our own ideas, thoughts, words and images because they can no longer express what is in our hearts. Silent prayer is a perfectly normal development of prayer and should not be thought to be at all unusual. It should never be our only way of prayer. We always say prayers especially when we gather together with other Christians; there is always need for some reflection in our lives and we need to feel free to respond to God from our hearts. However there does come a time when silence is the only adequate human response to God. In every life there will be moments of silence when words are inadequate but there is a time when we may be called to adopt silence as our normal way of prayer. This is never an empty silence but one that is filled with God. It is important to respond to God's call, not jumping the gun but neither ignoring the call.

Silence is not an end in itself. Exterior silence is of value only in so far as it leads beyond itself and opens the door of the heart into interior silence. One of the best ways to avoid making progress in the spiritual journey is to fill our days with frenetic activity under the pretence that outer duties and cares are so pressing that we simply do not have time for prayer. If we do not take time to simply be in God's presence, we cannot expect to develop a deep relationship with God.

Some people cannot understand what silent prayer is. So let us be clear. Silent prayer does not mean having a blank mind. There is nothing valuable in having a blank mind - indeed it could be very dangerous. As Thomas Merton wrote, "An emptiness that is deliberately cultivated, for the sake of fulfilling a personal spiritual ambition, is not empty at all: it is full of itself. It is so full that the light of God cannot get into it anywhere...."[93] Also a stone has no thoughts but who wants to be a stone? Since we are human, we cannot help having thoughts and indeed we should rejoice in being able to have thoughts since they prove that we are alive. However, in prayer we relate to God who is far, far greater than our thoughts. We cannot capture God and put Him in the straight jacket of our thoughts, ideas and feelings. So any feeling of God's presence, no matter how wonderful it may seem to be is most certainly not God. It may or may not come from God so the best way of dealing with it

---

[93] *Contemplative Prayer*, Image Books, Doubleday, New York, 1990, p.94

is to let it come and let it go. If I try to hold on to it, I am turning away from God and focusing instead on my experience. At the beginning of a relationship with God it is right and necessary to reflect but our reflections do not confine God. At some point we need to be quiet, be still, so that God can speak to our hearts.

When we try to be quiet, lots of thoughts immediately crowd into our minds. Usually we can recognise them as distractions. The best way to deal with distractions is not to fight them because then our whole prayer will be one long battle. The best way I believe is simply to let them go i.e. not chase after them to beat them into submission or oppose them or try to grasp hold of them but simply let them go.

If you feel called to move beyond your own thoughts and meditations and simply rest in God, follow that inspiration. When you go to a foreign country, you may understand nothing at first and that can be quite frustrating but gradually you will begin to recognise some words and then phrases. You have to stay with it and not give up. If you feel called to enter into silence, stay with it or rather stay with God who reveals Himself in the silence. When you begin to hear the silent music, no other music will satisfy you.

For any successful human relationship, we must take time simply to be with the other and listen deeply to the other. However, we are not very good at really listening. We hear what we want to hear; we filter what is said to us through the sieve of our own agenda. We have difficulty hearing the other because of the constant noise inside ourselves. If we do this in daily life, we do it also at the time of prayer. Part of the transformation process is that our human and therefore limited ways of thinking and loving must be transformed into divine ways. When we read or meditate or even when we speak spontaneously to God, we are in control and it is very difficult for us to let go so that God can take over. Lectio Divina moves towards silence. When our words and our beautiful thoughts are no longer sufficient, only silence can give an adequate response to the Word of God.

Silence is of course not just when we do not vocalise words. Exterior silence is not necessarily the same as interior silence. We should not assume that silence will come naturally to us. We have to learn how to be silent.

The purpose of silent prayer is not to create an empty mind; the purpose is to quieten down the noise within us so that we can truly hear what God desires to say to us. We can listen to God by thinking and reflecting on the Word but our reflection is always in some way moulded by our unrecognised hidden motivations. When we take a break from our own ways of thinking, we can give a space for God's ways of thinking to enter our lives and mould our hearts so that we begin to see as God sees and love as God loves. No matter how holy our reflections may seem to be, we will never think our way to transformation. This is the work of God and we need to give God space to accomplish this great work.

The core concept of the Carmelite way of following Christ is contemplation. This term can cause difficulties because of the way it has been used and abused over the centuries. Due to misinterpretations, the idea of contemplation was marginalized in the Church, and anyone who aspired to grow in his or her relationship with God was often told to play safe and stick with discursive meditation. Fixed methods of discursive meditation seem to be unfashionable nowadays. Instead there are several methods of silent prayer that have attracted many people. Some of these methods are based on Eastern religious practices and some come from the Christian contemplative tradition. Fidelity to such a practice can lead people relatively quickly to ask questions about the activity of God in the human heart. Carmelite spirituality, with its focus on contemplation, provides solid food for the spiritual journey and does provide great help to one who is seeking a deeper life in God.

Progress in prayer is normally characterised by the gradual transformation of many words and thoughts into the simplicity of loving surrender. As our prayer life matures, we become increasingly more disinclined towards a multiplicity of discursive acts and ever more inclined towards the wordless, imageless loving receptivity of contemplation. Our stance before God becomes simply that of 'here I am'.

The mere absence of thoughts, emotions, activity or distractions does not constitute prayer of any kind. A fruitful silence is one that is filled with desire for God; it is not an absence of words or thoughts but the expression of a heart for which words and thoughts are no longer adequate to express its love.

Silent prayer is of very great help in increasing the spirit of contemplation. We need to give an adequate time to prayer. Each individual has to decide what is an adequate time in the circumstances of his or her own life. There can be no hard and fast rules imposed from outside to an intimate relationship of friendship. However if we are too busy to pray, then we are too busy. The stage of contemplatio, in the Lectio Divina way of prayer, is where we let go of our own limited ways of praying for a short period and allow God to act in us. So we are invited to simply rest in God beyond words, beyond thoughts, beyond our activity. When or if this silence becomes contemplation is best left in God's hands. However in the silence we slowly learn a new language that transcends our poor limited human words and then silence becomes far more eloquent than many words.

What happens when we let go of our pious words and thoughts? We find ourselves thinking of what is for lunch or having an internal argument with someone who has wronged us in the past. When we become aware of this, we may very well feel that this silent prayer business is not for us, that we cannot do it and that we had better stick to meditation where we have something to occupy our busy minds. I suggest that this reaction, while understandable, is mistaken. What really matters in our prayer is not our words or thoughts, important though these are, but our *desire*. What do you really desire? As you know it is very possible for the lips to say one thing and for the heart to say the opposite. God reads the heart; God knows the desire of our heart even though our minds may seem to be far away. Obviously when we become aware that we are distracted, we can choose to continue thinking about lunch or whatever but that would be changing our intention of simply being in God's presence. It is better just to renew our intention to be in God's presence and to be open to God's action and we can do so in many ways, for example by the use of a simple word or even an interior glance towards God. It may be that the use of many words or even holy thoughts is not helpful at this time. We have all had the experience in a human relationship where silence speaks far more eloquently than many words. Even very busy people can maintain intimate human relationships and so in the midst of our busy lives we are invited into an intimate relationship with God. Indeed with this relationship at the centre of our lives, all our activity will become much more fruitful.

The process of contemplation changes the human ways of thinking, loving and acting into divine ways. Our human ways are very limited and so when we read the Word of God, we are limited by our experience of life and by many other factors. It is said that one can find in the Bible reasons to support any position. It is therefore not sufficient just to read the Bible; our way of looking at things must be purified. When we meditate on the Word of God, we try to understand its meaning and what message it may have for our lives but when we do this, we are still limited. Our little world must be enlarged and our minds reformed according to the mind of Christ. When we pray from the heart, we are still using human words. Our words and thoughts, no matter how beautiful, are still human words and thoughts and it is therefore necessary that they too be purified by the Word of God.

The process of transformation normally takes place in and through all the events of daily life. John of the Cross calls the first part of this process of transformation, the night of sense which is only the beginning. The real purification and transformation takes place in the second part of the night, the darkest part but closer to the dawn. The dark night is a blessing because it is an effect of the process of contemplation, which is an inflow of God into the soul. God is light but the light is so brilliant that it appears to be darkness to the human being.

God speaks in the silence

God speaks to us in the silence of the night. In concrete terms what actually happens when we experience silence? Often we feel rather uncomfortable because we are not used to silence. Our world is filled with noise – radio, television, constant chatting about this and that – words, words, words. When we pray, we do not change our human nature and so for this reason we may find silence difficult even at times of prayer. There exists the temptation even to fill the entire experience of Lectio Divina with words. Of course it is necessary to take time to read the Word of God, to meditate on it and to pray it with words and thoughts, which arise spontaneously from our hearts but it is equally important to leave space for silence where we simply listen for the voice of God.

The voice of God is so gentle that we run the risk of suffocating it with the noise within ourselves. Consciously we need to enter into silence and, leaving aside our beautiful words and holy thoughts for a moment, we reserve a space, which we hope God will fill.

The silence to which I am referring is not merely an empty space, a lack of words; it is a desire to which God alone can respond. There is a type of silence that is not Christian. Everything depends on one's intention. If we want to use the time of silence to sleep or daydream or for relaxation, that is not Christian prayer. It is, however, possible to enter into silence with the best of intentions and after a few minutes to fall asleep or become distracted but if our intention is to communicate with God, Father, Son and Holy Spirit, it remains prayer. To appreciate the value of silence, we must be convinced that God lives and works in us whether we are awake or asleep. God does not need our beautiful words and holy thoughts but our desire. If we really desire that God transform us, He will do it. However it is possible to use words and thoughts in order to stay just as we are but to feel that we are really making headway on the spiritual journey.

Centering Prayer

There are various methods that can help us to become silent when we pray and to remain in silence. Without some sort of method, we could not continue to be silent for long. Our normal waking consciousness is filled with thoughts – one follows another in an unending stream. When we try to create a silent interior space in order that we might listen to God, immediately all sorts of distractions try to lead us away from our focus. It is very difficult to focus our attention totally on God. Within a few minutes we will find ourselves thinking what is for lunch or something else equally important. One way to avoid being distracted is not to try to focus our attention at all but instead to focus our intention on God. If at the beginning of my time of prayer, I formulate an intention to be in the presence of God and to invite God to transform me, that intention is not changed simply because I am distracted. A distraction can change the focus of my attention but not my intention. I only change my intention if I willingly follow a distraction. Whenever I become aware of being distracted, I simply renew my intention to be in the presence of God and to be transformed by the action of God.

In order to remain focused on God in silence, I believe that we need some method of prayer. Otherwise we can spend a fairly pleasant time just daydreaming but that is not prayer. A way of prayer, which I have found useful, Centering Prayer, based on the classic "Cloud of Unknowing",[94] stresses the letting go of all thoughts. Thoughts is an umbrella term for any perception at all including all feelings, images, memories, reflections, commentaries and so on. What about holy thoughts and feelings? What if in the middle of my prayer period I have the most powerful feeling of God's presence? Why should I not ponder on that? Ponder on it if you like but in doing so you are taking a step backwards. Some people like to experience a beautiful sunset and other people like to take photographs of it.

Centering Prayer is a method of Christian prayer based on the very rich Christian contemplative tradition. If one is praying at all,

---

[94] Anon, *Cloud of Unknowing* and Other Works, trans. C. Wolters, (London, Penguin Books, 1961)

one is using some method of prayer, whether from a traditional source or from one's own ingenuity. The method which I am proposing is not intended to replace whatever method one is using but it can make other ways of prayer more fruitful. This method has helped me greatly and I simply want to share it. The most important thing for this method of prayer is to be convinced that God is not far away but in fact is very near. God has set up home in our hearts.

This method of prayer can be called the prayer of silence or the prayer of desire but it is most often called Centering Prayer.[95] In the silence we tend towards God with our desire. It is a very simple way of listening to God but its very simplicity can be deceptive. Centering Prayer assumes a growing relationship with God and particularly regular contact with God through Sacred Scripture. It prepares us to hear the voice of God, to encounter God, as the Prophet Elijah did, in the sound of sheer silence (1 Kings, 19, 11-13).

Centering prayer helps us to be silent and prepares us for the gift of contemplation when and as God desires to give us this gift. Contemplation is pure gift and cannot be merited in any way nor can it be brought on by any clever method. Terms have tended to be used very loosely and I do not think that it is helpful to do so. Often silent prayer has been called contemplative prayer. However, in the western Christian tradition, contemplation or contemplative prayer occurs when God intervenes and takes over completely. At such moments we can do nothing except experience what God wishes us to experience. God enters by a secret door unknown to us. It is like a house with three rooms. You can move from the first to the second through the adjoining door but you cannot move into the third room because there is no door. Indeed there is no evidence that there is a third room except that previous occupants have been there. You cannot go into the third room; you can only be brought there. You are not aware of going in; you just find yourself there - how you know not.

So centering prayer is not contemplative prayer but is a way to do everything we can to be ready for God. True contemplation will

---

[95] Centering Prayer was taught originally by three Trappist monks in the USA who had made a profound study of the Christian Contemplative Tradition. The basic book to learn more about this way of prayer is by Thomas Keating OCSO, *Open Mind, Open Heart. The Contemplative Dimension of the Gospel*, Element Books, Mass., USA, 1992. For a simple introduction to Centering Prayer and its background, see E. Smith & J. Chalmers, *A Deeper Love*, (Burns & Oates & Continuum, U.K. & USA), 1999

have wonderful effects in our lives but the test of whether we truly are growing in the love of God is whether we are growing in the love of neighbour. Wonderful experiences in prayer are no substitute for a practical down to earth care and concern for others.

There are four very simple guidelines to this prayer. First of all try to find a place where interruptions will be reduced to a minimum, then get yourself into a comfortable position which you can maintain for the whole period of prayer. The position should not be so comfortable that we fall asleep, even though God loves us whether we are awake or asleep! A minimum of twenty minutes is recommended. To set the mood, one could begin by reading a small portion of Scripture. We do not want to think of the meaning of these words; meditation is for another time. We desire only to be in the presence of God and to consent to God's action. This is not a prayer of attention but intention.[96]

After having quietened down, the next step of this simple way of prayer is to close one's eyes and silently introduce a sacred word into one's consciousness. A sacred word is a word that has great significance for you in your relationship with God but it need not be a traditionally "holy" word. Take the example of the little word "yes". It can mean very little or a great deal depending on the circumstances and the intention of the person speaking. The word that you choose should be sacred for you. According to the teaching of the 'Cloud of Unknowing", it is better if the word you choose be brief, one syllable if possible. I can suggest some possible words:- "God, Lord, Abba, Father, Spirit, Jesus, Mary, Yes, Peace, Love, Joy".

When I say, "introduce the sacred word into one's consciousness", I do not mean to pronounce the word aloud or even silently in one's mind but to allow the word to rise up within oneself without pondering on its meaning. It is not necessary to use great mental force with this word; it is introduced very, very gently. The sacred word is not a mantra; it is not repeated continually during the prayer but is used only when necessary, when we find that we are thinking of something else instead of simply being in the presence of God and consenting to God's action. The sacred word renews our intention and we use it always in the same way to return our heart to the Lord when we become aware that we are thinking of anything else. Our intention is simply to be in the presence of God and consent to God's

---

[96] For an explanation of the use of will and intention in Centering Prayer, see T. Keating, *Intimacy with God*, (Crossroad, New York, 1994)

action in our lives. Our sacred word expresses our intention and so when we become aware that we are thinking of something, we can decide either to continue thinking about whatever we became aware of or to return to our original intention of simply being in God's presence and consenting to God's action. This we do by re-introducing ever so gently the sacred word that we have chosen.

During the period of this prayer, it is not the time to speak to God in words or have holy thoughts. We can do all this at another time. Our silence and our desire are worth much more than many words.

By means of the sacred word that we have chosen, we express our desire and our intention to remain in the presence of God and to consent to God's purifying and transforming action. We return to the sacred word, which is the symbol of our intention and desire, only when we are aware that we are thinking about something else. There is no point in getting upset at our distractions, because that is just another thought, but we return very gently to our sacred word as the symbol of our intention to remain in God's presence and to submit to and co-operate with God's action in our lives. The prayer itself consists simply in being in the presence of God without thinking of anything in particular. It is a prayer of relationship with God, Father, Son and Holy Spirit. If we understand how to be with another person in silence without doing anything else, then we can understand this prayer. This method of prayer can be helpful to those who feel within themselves a call to silence.

Practical guidelines for Centering Prayer

There are four simple guidelines to the method of Centering Prayer. These are:-

1. Choose a Sacred Word as the symbol of your intention to consent to the presence and action of God within.

2. Sitting comfortably and with eyes closed, settle briefly and silently introduce the Sacred Word as the symbol of your intention to consent to God's presence and action.

3. When you become aware of thoughts return ever so gently to the Sacred Word

4. At the end of the prayer period, remain in silence for a few minutes with eyes closed.

CHAPTER SIX

MARY THE CONTEMPLATIVE

In the Gospels Mary is presented to us as a model. She is the woman of faith, the perfect disciple of Jesus Christ. Mary was a contemplative, which does not mean that she spent all day on her knees. A contemplative is a mature friend of God who looks upon reality as if with the eyes of God and loves what she sees as if with God's heart.

After the stunning news that she received at the Annunciation, Our Lady hurried to visit Elizabeth who told her that she was blessed because of her faith. God does not require us to do very difficult things or great things. God wants to do great things in and through us. Mary co-operated with the Word of God and so gave God space to work in her life. She was blessed not principally for what she did but because of what God had done in her.

The hidden agenda

She listened to the Word of God; she pondered everything in her heart; she thought about what happened to her and what was said to her and she was able to discern the voice of God in the midst of her day-to-day reality. Like Mary, we are called to be contemplatives. We are called to contemplatively listen to the Word of God no matter how it comes to us. Our Lady had no barriers in her to the accomplishment of God's will. Therefore she knew how to listen. We must learn how to listen. In order to be able to listen to God, we must be aware of our own hidden agenda. A hidden agenda is the collection of prejudices and ideas that really motivate much of what we do and say despite what we may believe to the contrary. These things are hidden very often from ourselves and sometimes from other people. At times what is motivating us is as clear as day to other people while remaining hidden from ourselves. For example some people pray in order to try to manipulate God into doing their will; they may say a lot of prayers but never give God an opportunity to speak to their hearts. Other people are afraid of God and have not accepted the fundamental point of the Gospel that God loves each one of us. They pray in order to placate a god who is always ready to crush them for the slightest infringement of the rules. Some may adhere very strictly to the rules and regulations because their faith is very weak and they may feel that without these props, they have nothing.

Another hidden agenda is the insecurity of needing to earn God's love, of not accepting it for what it is – a completely unmerited free gift from God. God does not look for good people who are worthy to receive divine love. God searches for men and women who will open their hearts and who will allow God to transform their lives, and through them to transform the life of the world. Some people, despite what they say, cannot believe that love is free. Perhaps because of their own experience, they have learned that love is conditional and they have imposed this past experience on God. Therefore such people feel the need to earn God's love, to merit it in some way. They can bolster a very weak self-image by looking down on other people, by deploring their weaknesses and denouncing their sins.

Prayer of course is very important but the test of the authenticity of prayer is how we live in daily life. Even prayer can be used as an escape from reality. The reality that surrounds us is the place of the encounter with the Living God. This reality can be difficult; it can be challenging but nevertheless it is the sacred space where we meet God. Prayer is not just bombarding God with requests and petitions; it is above all an opening of our hearts, our lives, to God. God has a plan for us and for our world and this plan is borne out of love for us. God does not impose on us but invites us to be co-workers in making the divine plan a reality in our world. We cannot pray with sincerity "Your Kingdom come" unless we seek to bring the values of the Kingdom to our own little part of the world and to allow these values to shape our own lives.

In prayer we invite God into our lives to shape and mould our hearts so that we can be instruments of God's peace and love, so that we can be tabernacles of God's presence. Jesus himself gave us the model of all prayer. God is Father of all and therefore all of us are members of the same family. We bless and thank God because by our faith we have grasped something of the divine plan for us and therefore we desire that God's will be done. Mary was eager that God's will be accomplished and she was more than willing to play her part. This eagerness for God's will remained unchanged despite the sufferings that came to her because of her acceptance. She proved that her prayer really was an opening to God by her acceptance and active co-operation with God's will.

The faith of Mary

When Mary looked into her own soul, she saw no trace of sin. She did not become proud but instead she thanked God who had "looked upon the lowliness of His handmaid". (Lk.1,48). She knew that all generations would call her blessed because the Almighty had done great things in her. In order for us to truly listen to God, we must seek to be aware of the barriers that we have within us. Our hidden agenda can act like a filter keeping out what we do not want to hear. We need to accept that our God is a God of surprises. Our Lady could have been forgiven if she had visualised a life of glory for herself as the mother of the long-awaited messiah but that did not happen. The birth of the messiah took place in poverty. Simeon warned her that a sword would pierce her soul; she had to flee to Egypt as a refugee; she heard from Jesus himself that it was not the physical relationship with him that made a person pleasing to God but the fact that one heard the Word of God and put it into practice. Finally she stood at the foot of the cross sharing in her Son's pain as he died seemingly a failure except to those who looked on him with the eyes of faith. In order to do God's will she had to accept the surprising ways God acted.

If our God is predictable and we always know what is God's will, then we are fooling ourselves. We must follow Jesus, not attempt to drag him along behind us. We must seek God's will by pondering the Word in our hearts as Mary did. So we must expect to be surprised by God. God will speak to us through the Scriptures, through the events of our day and through the events within the society of which we are part. In order to hear the Word of God for us, we must seek to purify our own hidden agenda which filters what God is saying so that we only hear what we want to hear. We need to ask God to reveal this hidden agenda to us perhaps bit by bit, as we are ready to accept it and to gradually change our motivation from self-gratification to a pure love of God and neighbour. We must give God the time and the space to speak to our hearts. Therefore at times we must be silent, pondering God's Word in our hearts as Mary did.

Our Lady is the model of what it means to follow Christ. By her eager and active co-operation, the Word of God took flesh in her and she brought forth Christ for the world. The Word of God must take flesh in us too. We have to make Christ present once again in our own time and place. We are to be co-workers with Christ in God's plan of salvation for humanity.

Mary's role in God's plan was of course unique. She gave birth to God's only Son but then for about thirty years nothing much happened. Jesus grew up but he did not preach or do anything spectacular. When he finally began his public ministry, Our Lady did not play a major role. It was only at the end when she stood at the foot of the cross that once again she played a clearly important role when she became the spiritual mother of humanity. All the bits in between, all those silent years, were important too. Mary needed faith to recognise them as important and to cling on to God, believing that God would fulfil all His promises in God's time.

We are asked to be faithful to God in our own particular situation. We are asked to live the Gospel where we are. We are asked to be contemplatives at the heart of the world, being aware of God's presence not in dramatic ways but in the midst of our ordinary everyday lives. Each of us then will be a focus for God's presence in our own little part of the world – rather like lightening conductors. We need to be aware of the presence of God within us and then in the people we meet. This awareness is not felt in any way but is an act of faith. God lives at the centre of each human being no matter what that person is like. As we become more and more aware of God's presence everywhere, we become more sensitive to the signs of the presence of God's Kingdom. The Hebrew Scriptures and especially the psalms speak of watchmen on the towers. They would be the first to see the dawn of a new day from their high positions. We are to be "Kingdom spotters", in that we will be able to recognise the values of the Kingdom in unlikely situations. Many people with no obvious religious affiliation live by the values of God's Kingdom, the same values that Jesus lived by and taught. We will be able to spot these even in the most unlikely people and encourage these values wherever we meet them. The visit of the poor shepherds to the crib and what they said made Our Lady ponder in her heart. She recognised the hand of God at work.

The meaning of our lives lies in allowing God to make us into what God knows we can be. Through us God wants to bring to fulfilment the plan of salvation for the whole human race and for the whole of creation. Our Lady was the God-bearer to the world for through her God became Emmanuel, one of us. She was not just a vessel for God to use. She actively co-operated with God by her loving faith. According to Blessed Titus Brandsma, the Carmelite is to be another Mary, another God-bearer for our world. God becomes present through us to other people and we allow God to touch others by our loving faith.

Mary is our Sister, accompanying us on our journey of faith, sharing with us the joys and sorrows of life. She is our Mother, nurturing the life of God within us. She prays with us and for us that we may become mature friends of God. Wearing the scapular expresses our commitment to Our Lady and her commitment to us.

Let it be a continual reminder to us of Mary's gentle presence in our lives, assisting us to become what we are called to be.

We experience ourselves as part of a world, which is full of contradictions. Our world is plagued by wars, famine and hatred. It is difficult to see any good coming out of horrible events like the terrorist attacks in the USA, yet people of faith need to be on the look out for signs of hope, sometimes only little seeds, but these signs give us encouragement and strength to continue to work, and above all trust, in the face of what can often seem to be impossible odds.

Contemplation begins when we entrust ourselves to God, whatever way God chooses to come to us. However we need to stay awake and recognise the approach of God who may come to us in totally unexpected ways. Mary received the Word of God through the message of an angel but was also open to hearing God's voice at the foot of the cross. Elijah met God not in the earthquake or the fire or the mighty wind but in the sound of sheer silence. (I Kings 19,11-13)

Can we discover the presence of God everywhere even in the midst of our world, which at times can be full of evil? This is the faith of Our Lady in the Magnificat who praises God for throwing down the proud, feeding the hungry and sending the rich away empty when most people would see the opposite as true. A contemplative is able to see beyond the externals to the reality beneath. A constant attitude of openness to God is of course not easy because the presence of God calls into question how we live and constantly calls us to conversion, which means change and we are not always very keen to change.

If we accept God's invitation to begin this interior journey, we will of course meet with difficulties on the way because we will be brought face to face with ourselves. We will see ever more clearly the motives for our actions. We will see that sometimes even our best actions have selfish motives. This is very difficult to accept and this is why the spiritual journey is so difficult and why many might want to turn back to a less challenging place. If, however we but knew the gift God was offering us, we would continue our journey despite the painful revelations about ourselves which we were offered. On this journey we become less proud, less sure of our own virtue but more reliant on the mercy of God and more aware that all human beings are our brothers and sisters.

Our world is undergoing great cultural upheaval as we begin the new millennium. There is a profound spiritual crisis in our times. What have we to say in this situation? The call to be contemplative is a vocation that affects the world. Contemplatives can be found in every walk of life. To be a contemplative is to respond in faith to a call from God who often seems to be hidden. In the midst of conflict and division, such people are tabernacles of God's presence, through whom God is powerfully present. Therefore in the present situation of our world, we can use whatever skills we have been given for the good of others but, above all, we can respond to the still small voice that calls us into an intimate relationship with Jesus Christ, the only Son of the Father. This is not a cosy intimacy but through the relationship with God, we will be gradually transformed to become what God knows we can be and be totally available for the divine work in the world. Mary was totally available for God. She is our model, our Mother and our Sister, accompanying us and encouraging us to believe always in God's promises, especially when appearances seem most discouraging.

What does a transformed person look like? Much depends on the personality of the individual of course. The divine shines through the human but the human is still present. The transformed person reflects without distortion some aspect of God. The road is long and we may never finish the journey in this life but it is vital at least to be on the journey. The spiritual journey leads to total freedom and to the fulfilment of that for which we were created. "Eye has not seen nor has ear heard, nor has the human heart conceived, what God has in store for those who love Him." (I Cor.2,9)

LETTER OF HIS HOLINESS POPE JOHN PAUL II FOR THE CARMELITE MARIAN YEAR

To the Most Reverend Fathers
JOSEPH CHALMERS
Prior General of the Order of the Brothers
Of the Blessed Virgin Mary of Mount Carmel (O.Carm.)
And
CAMILO MACCISE
Prepositus General of the Order of the Discalced Brothers
Of the Blessed Virgin Mary of Mount Carmel (O.C.D.)

1. The Jubilee Year, which was a providential event of grace for the Church, leads her to look with trust and hope at the journey into the third millennium, which has just begun. I wrote in the Apostolic Letter, *Novo millennio ineunte*, "At the beginning of this new century, our steps must quicken. On this journey we are accompanied by the Blessed Virgin Mary to whom I entrusted the Third Millennium" (no. 58)

With profound joy I have been made aware that the Order of Carmel, in both its branches, ancient and reformed, desires to express its filial love towards its Patroness by dedicating the year 2001 to Her, who is invoked as the Flower of Carmel, Mother and Guide on the path of holiness. In this regard, I could not fail to underline a happy coincidence: the celebration of this Marian year for the whole of Carmel takes place, according to a venerable tradition of the Order itself, in the 750th anniversary of the giving of the Scapular. Therefore it is a celebration that constitutes for the entire Carmelite Family a marvellous occasion to deepen not only its Marian spirituality, but to live it more and more in the light of the place that the Virgin Mother of God and our Mother occupies in the mystery of Christ and the Church. In this way, you can follow Her who is the "Star of the New Evangelisation" (Cf. *Novo millennio ineunte*, n.58)

2. Generations of Carmelites, from the beginnings up to today, in their journey towards the "holy mountain, Jesus Christ Our Lord" (Roman Missal, Collect for the Mass in honour of the BVM of Mt. Carmel, 16 July), have sought to model their lives after the example of Mary.

For this reason, contemplation of the Blessed Virgin flourishes in Carmel and in every soul moved by a tender affection towards Her who is our most holy Mother. From the very beginning, she knew how to be open to the Word of God and obedient to God's will (Lk.2,19.51). Mary, who was educated and formed by the Spirit (cf. Lk. 2,44-50), was able to read her own life experience in the light of faith (cf. Lk. 1, 46-55). She was docile to the divine promptings and "advanced in her pilgrimage of faith, and loyally persevered in her union with her Son unto the cross. There she stood in keeping with the divine plan (cf. Jn. 19,25), suffering grievously with her only-begotten Son. There she united herself with a maternal heart to His sacrifice" (*Lumen gentium*, 58).

3. The contemplation of the Blessed Virgin shows her as the attentive Mother who watches her Son growing up in Nazareth (cf. Lk. 2,40.52), and follows him along the roads of Palestine. We see her at the wedding feast of Cana (cf. Jn.2,5) and at the foot of the Cross, where she became the Mother of all, associated with the self offering of her Son and given to all people when Jesus Himself gave Her to the beloved disciple (cf. Jn. 19,26). As Mother of the Church, the Holy Virgin is united with the disciples "in continuous prayer" (Acts 1,14) and, as the New Woman assumed into heaven, she anticipates in herself that which one day will come to pass for all of us in the full enjoyment of the life of the Trinity. Assumed into heaven, She now extends the protective mantle of her mercy over her children who are still on pilgrimage towards the holy mountain of glory.

A similar contemplative attitude of mind and heart brings us to admire the Blessed Virgin's faith and love, by which She already possesses what every faithful Christian desires and hopes to be within the mystery of Christ and the Church (cf. *Sacrosanctum Concilium, 103; Lumen gentium, 53*). For this reason, Carmelites justly have chosen Mary as their Patroness and spiritual Mother and keep her always in mind, She who is the Most Pure Virgin and who leads all to the perfect knowledge and imitation of Christ.

In this way a spiritual intimacy develops in which the communion with Christ and with Mary is always growing. For the members of the Carmelite Family, Mary, the Virgin Mother of God and Mother of all people, is not only a model to imitate, but is also present as Mother and Sister in whom one can confide. Rightly St. Teresa of Jesus wrote, "Imitate Mary and consider how great she must be and what a good thing it is that we have her for our Patroness" (*Interior Castle, III, 1, 3*).

4. This intense Marian life, which is expressed in trusting prayer, in enthusiastic praise and in diligent imitation, leads us to understand that the most genuine form of devotion to the Most Holy Virgin, expressed by the humble sign of the Scapular, is the consecration to her Immaculate Heart (cf. Letter of Pope Pius XII, *Neminem profecto latet* [11 February 1950: AAS 42, 1950, pp. 390-391]; Dogmatic Constitution on the Church *Lumen gentium*, 67). Therefore in each one's heart a communion and familiarity with the Holy Virgin grows, "as a new way of living for God and continuing here on earth the love which Jesus had towards his mother Mary" (cf. *Sermon at the Angelus, in Insegnamenti XI/3, 1988, p.173*). In this way, according to the expression of the Blessed martyr Titus Brandsma, we are profoundly united with Mary, the *Theotokos*, becoming like her, bearers of the divine life: "The Lord sends an angel also to us...... we also must receive God in our hearts, carry him in our hearts, nourish him and let him grow within us so that he is born from us and lives with us as Emmanuel, God-with-us (*From the talk of Bl. Titus Brandsma to the Mariological Congress of Tongerloo, August 1936*).

This rich Marian heritage which Carmel possesses has become over time a treasure for the whole Church, through the spread of the devotion of the Brown Scapular. By means of its simplicity, its relatedness to ordinary human life and its connection with the role of Mary in the Church and the whole of humanity, this devotion has been profoundly and whole heartedly received by the people of God, so much so as to be remembered in the memorial of 16th July, which is in the liturgical calendar of the Universal Church.

5. The Scapular represents a synthesis of Marian spirituality. It nourishes the devotion of believers, making them sensitive to the loving presence of the Virgin Mother in their lives. The Scapular is essentially a "habit". Those who receive it are aggregated or associated in varying degrees with the Order of Carmel, which is dedicated to the service of Our Lady for the good of the whole Church (cf. *Formula for the imposition of the Scapular*, in the "Rite of Blessing and imposition of the Scapular", approved by the Congregation for Divine Worship and the Discipline of the Sacraments, 5/1/1996). Those who put on the Scapular are introduced into the land of Carmel so that they might "eat its abundant fruit" (cf. Jer. 2,7), and experience the tender and maternal presence of Mary, as they commit themselves daily to put on Christ and to make his presence manifest in their lives for the good of the Church and of the whole of humanity (cf. *Formula for the imposition of the Scapular*, cit).

There are two truths which the sign of the Scapular brings out:

on the one hand, there is the continuous protection of the Blessed Virgin, not only along the pathways of this life, but also at the moment of passing into the fullness of eternal glory; on the other hand, there is the awareness that devotion towards Our Lady cannot be limited to the occasional prayer in her honour, but must become a "habit", that is a permanent way of Christian living, made up of prayer and the interior life, frequent recourse to the Sacraments and the concrete exercise of the corporal and spiritual works of mercy. In this way the Scapular becomes a sign of "covenant" and of reciprocal communion between Mary and the faithful. It expresses in a concrete way the gift, which Jesus, while hanging on the cross, made of his Mother to John, and through him to us. It also gives expression to Jesus' commitment of the beloved disciple and us to Her, who thus became our spiritual Mother.

6. The witness of holiness and wisdom of so many Saints of Carmel, who all grew up under the shade and the care of their Mother, is a splendid example of this Marian spirituality, which forms us and configures us to Christ, who is the first born among many brothers and sisters.

For a very long time I too have worn the Carmelite Scapular! Because of the love which I have for our heavenly Mother, whose protection I experience constantly, I wish that this Marian year be an aid to all the religious in Carmel and the faithful who venerate her, to grow in their love of Her and to radiate in the world the presence of this Woman of silence and of prayer, who is invoked as the Mother of mercy, the Mother of hope and of grace.

With these wishes, I gladly impart the Apostolic Blessing to all the friars, nuns, sisters and lay members of the Carmelite Family, who work so hard to spread among the people of God the true devotion to Mary, Star of the Sea and Flower of Carmel!

The Vatican, 25th March 2001

Joannes Paulus II

The Rule of Saint Albert

Paragraph numbers are in square brackets to indicate that they are not part of the original Rule. *They were agreed by the General Councils of both Carmelite Orders and published in 1999. The additions of Pope Innocent IV 1247, when he approved St. Albert's "Formula vitae", and make it officially a Rule, are given in italics. The translation is by Kees Waaijman and can be found in his book,* The Mystical Space of Carmel, *(Peeters, Leuven, 1999), p.29-38. This book was published before the agreement for the new numbering and therefore follows the old numbering.*

[1]

Albert by the grace of God called to be Patriarch of the Church of Jerusalem, to his beloved sons in Christ, B. and the other hermits who are living under obedience to him at the spring on Mount Carmel: salvation in the Lord and the blessing of the Holy Spirit.

[2]

In many and various ways the holy fathers have laid down how everyone, whatever their state of life or whatever kind of religious life he has chosen, should live in allegiance to Jesus Christ and serve him faithfully from a pure heart and a good conscience.

[3]

However, because you desire us to give you a formula of life in keeping with your purpose, to which you may hold fast in the future:

[4]

We establish first of all that you shall have one of you as prior, to be chosen for that office by the unanimous assent of all, or of the greater and wiser part, to whom each of the others shall promise obedience and strive to fulfil his promise by the reality of his deeds, *along with chastity and the renunciation of property.*

[5]

You may have places in solitary areas, or where you are given a site that is suitable and convenient for the observance of your religious life, as the prior and the brothers see fit.

[6]

Next, according to the site of the place where you propose to dwell, each of you shall have a separate cell of his own, to be assigned to him by the disposition of the prior himself, with the assent of the other brothers or the wiser part of them.

[7]

However, you shall eat whatever may have been given you in a common refectory, listening together to some reading from Sacred Scripture, where this can be done conveniently.

[8]

None of the brothers may change the place assigned to him, or exchange it with another, except with the permission of whoever is prior at the time.

[9]

The prior's cell shall be near the entrance to the place, so that he may be the first to meet those who come to this place, and so that whatever needs to be done subsequently may all be carried out according to his judgement and disposition.

[10]

Let each remain in his cell or near it, meditating day and night on the Word of the Lord and keeping vigil in prayer, unless he is occupied with other lawful activities.

[11]

Those who know *how to say the canonical hours with the clerics* shall say *them according to* the institution of the Holy Fathers and the approved custom of the Church. Those who do not know their letters shall say twenty-five Our Fathers for the night vigil, except on Sundays and feastdays, for the vigils of which we establish that the stated number be doubled, so that the Our Father is said fifty times. The same prayer is to be said seven times for the morning lauds. For the other hours the same prayer is to be said seven times, except for the evening office, for which you shall say it fifteen times.

[12]

Let none of the brothers say that anything is his property, but let everything be held in common among you; to each one shall be distributed what he needs from the hand of the prior—that is from the *brother* he appoints to this task— taking into account the age and needs of each one.

[13]

You may, moreover, have asses or mules as your needs require, and some livestock or poultry for your nourishment.

[14]

An oratory, as far as it can be done conveniently, shall be built in the midst of the cells, where you shall come together every day early in the morning to hear Mass, where this can be done conveniently.

[15]

On Sundays too, or on other days when necessary, you shall discuss the preservation of order and the salvation of your souls. At this time also the excesses and faults of the brothers, if such should be found in anyone, should be corrected in the midst of love.

[16]

You shall observe the fast every day except Sunday from the feast of the Exaltation of the Holy Cross until Easter Sunday, unless sickness or bodily weakness or some other good reason shall make it advisable to break the fast; for necessity knows no law.

[17]

You shall abstain from meat, unless it be taken as a remedy for sickness or weakness. *And since you may have to beg more frequently while travelling, outside your own houses you may eat food cooked with meat, so as not to be a burden to your hosts. But meat may even be eaten at sea.*

[18]

However, because human life on earth is a trial, and all who wish to live devotedly in Christ must suffer persecution, and moreover since your adversary the devil, prowls around like a roaring lion seeking whom he may devour, you shall use every care and diligence to put on the armour of God, so that you may be able to withstand the deceits of the enemy.

[19]

The loins are to be girt with the cincture of chastity. Your breast is to be fortified with holy ponderings, for it is written: Holy ponderings will save you. The breastplate of justice is to be put on, that you may love the Lord your God with all your heart and all your soul and all your strength, and your neighbour as yourself. In all things is to be taken up the shield of faith, with which you will be able to quench all the flaming arrows of the wicked one, for without faith it is impossible to please God. On your head is to be put the helmet of salvation, that you may hope for salvation from the only Saviour who saves his people from their sins. And the sword of the Spirit, which is the word of God, should dwell abundantly in your mouth and in your hearts. And whatever you have to do, let it all be done in the Word of the Lord.

[20]

Some work has to be done by you, so that the devil may always find you occupied, lest on account of your idleness he manage to find some opportunity to enter into your souls. In this matter you have both the teaching and example of the blessed apostle Paul, in whose mouth Christ spoke, who was appointed and given by God as preacher and teacher of the nations in faith and truth; if you follow him you cannot go astray. Labouring and weary we lived among you, he says, working night and day so as not to be a burden to any of you; not that we had no right to do otherwise, but so as to give you ourselves as an example, that you might imitate us. For when we were with you we used to tell you, if someone is unwilling to work, let him not eat. For we have heard that there are certain people among you going about restlessly and doing no work. We urge people of this kind and beseech them in the Lord Jesus Christ to earn their bread, working in silence. *This way is holy and good: follow it.*

[21]

The apostle recommends silence, when he tells us to work in it. As the prophet also testifies, Silence is the cultivation of justice; and again, in silence and hope will be your strength.

Therefore we direct that you keep silence from after *compline* until *prime* of the following day.

At other times, however, although you need not observe silence so strictly, you should nevertheless be all the more careful to avoid much talking, for as it is written—and experience teaches no less— where there is much talk sin will not be lacking; and, he who is careless in speech will come to harm; and elsewhere, he who uses many words injures his soul. And the Lord says in the gospel: For every idle word that people speak they will render account on judgement day. Let each one, therefore, measure his words and keep a tight rein on his mouth, lest he stumble and fall by his talking and his fall be irreparable and prove fatal. With the prophet let him watch his ways lest he sin with his tongue; let him try attentively and carefully to practice the silence in which is the cultivation of justice.

[22]

And you, brother B., and whoever may be appointed prior after you, should always have in mind and observe in practice what the Lord says in the gospel: Whoever wishes to be the greatest among you will be your servant, and whoever wishes to be the first will be your slave.

[23]

You other brothers too, hold your prior humbly in honour, thinking not so much of him as of Christ who placed him over you, and who said to the leaders of the churches, Who hears you hears me; who rejects you rejects me. In this way you will not come into judgement for contempt, but through obedience will merit the reward of eternal life.

[24]

We have written these things briefly for you, thus establishing a formula for your way of life, according to which you are to live. If anyone will have spent more, the Lord himself will reward him, when he returns. Use discernment, however, the guide of the virtues.